ANXIETY AND PERSONALITY

ANXIETY AND PERSONALITY

The Concept of a Directing Object and its Applications

Karl König

KARNAC

For ease of reading, "he" is used throughout for the patient (and the child) and "she" for the therapist, but, at any point, the opposite gender can be substituted.

First published in German in 2000

First published in English in 2015 by
Karnac Books Ltd
118 Finchley Road
London NW3 5HT

British Library Cataloguing in Publication Data

A C.I.P. for this book is available from the British Library

ISBN-13: 978-1-78220-040-6

Typeset by V Publishing Solutions Pvt Ltd., Chennai, India

Printed in Great Britain

www.karnacbooks.com

CONTENTS

ABOUT THE AUTHOR

Karl König, MD, studied medicine at Heidelberg, where he became a medical doctor in 1957 and worked for several years in the Heidelberg Institute of Physiology. In Hamburg University he trained as an internist, and in Göttingen as a psychoanalyst. From 1971 to 1981 he directed the psychotherapy department for adults in a state hospital concentrating on neuroses, borderline conditions, and psychosomatic disturbances. At the medical school of Göttingen University he was then appointed director of a department concentrating on clinical group psychotherapy and couples therapy. More recently, his scientific work has addressed anxiety syndromes and problems of technique in psychoanalysis and psychotherapy. He has written or co-authored thirty-one books, which have been translated into several languages. He was president of the Göttingen psychoanalytic institute and vice president of the German Psychoanalytic Society, and is a member of the IPA.

PREFACE

In the German version this book has seen three editions and three reprints to date. In the second and third editions I had included addenda which I have now integrated into the main body of the book. Some of the references to literature which have proved of ephemeral interest have been omitted and I have amplified the sections of the book that address applications of the concept in practice.

The subject of this book is one that I originally discussed with Reinhard Kreische, Regine Tischtau-Schröter, and Ulrich Streeck. Regine Tischtau-Schröter also helped me to obtain the literature cited here. At a later stage I had fruitful discussions with Jochen Biskup, Gerlinde Herdieckerhoff-Sandler, Reinhard Kreische, Falk Leichsenring, and Hermann Staats, who worked with me in a department of clinical group psychotherapy at Göttingen University, and also with colleagues at the Lou Andreas Salomé Institute of Psychoanalysis and Psychotherapy: these were Mohammad Ephraim Ardjomandi, Jochen Haustein, Anne Heigl-Evers, Ursula Kreuzer-Haustein, and Wulf Volker Lindner. Franz Heigl appointed me to a post at the state hospital for psychotherapy and psychosomatics at Tiefenbrunn near Göttingen, which enabled me to see patients presented by six to seven collaborators who were also training to be psychoanalysts at the Göttingen institute.

I wish to express my thanks to all the colleagues mentioned and also to Dagmar Friedrich, from Vandenhoeck, and Ruprecht in Göttingen, who helped me to make the book more accessible, to Erika Dzimalle, who typed most of the manuscript, and to Barbara Kreer, who typed the remainder. I am also grateful to Natascha Faull, who helped me with the first English language version, and for the final revision of the text my thanks go to Harriet Hasenclever.

INTRODUCTION

In the course of the twelve years during which I worked at the Lower Saxony State Hospital at Tiefenbrunn—is a specialist clinic for psychogenic and psychosomatic disorders—I was repeatedly confronted with patients who were suffering from symptoms of anxiety. It struck me that these patients had certain characteristics in common and I began to look into the genesis and metapsychological foundations of these personality traits. This then led to the formulation of a concept of a phobic personality structure, which it is the intention of this book to illuminate, in describing how it arises, its unconscious roots, its psychodynamics, and the patients' subjective experience of it.

Theory

The theoretical basis of this book combines ego psychology with object relations theory, as conceptualised by Otto Kernberg (1975, 1976) in the United States, Joseph Sandler and Anne Marie Sandler (Sandler & Sandler, 1994), and, in addition, Fonagy, Cooper, and Wallerstein (1999) in the United Kingdom. I also participated in clinical workshops linking theory and practice conducted by Anne-Marie Sandler.

Clinical observations

This book is based on the study of about 3000 patients whose cases I explored during a period of ten years from 1971 to 1981. The colleague presenting a patient spent around half an hour recounting his or her findings. In the next step I had a conversation with the patient for about twenty minutes and a further ten minutes was given to discussing the way the patient was to be treated in individual or group therapy or in a combination of the two, supplemented by sports, art therapy, occupational therapy, or trial work experience in the nearby town of Göttingen. I saw the patients on my weekly rounds through the wards for a period of six weeks to six months, occasionally longer. Many patients could have been treated in an outpatient setting but were admitted to the hospital because there were not enough therapists where they lived. As a supervisor at the psychoanalytic institute I was able to follow the treatment of patients in analysis over several years.

About one quarter of the patients I came to know over the ten-year period showed anxiety as a symptom. They were for the main part suffering from phobias, and a majority of them were agoraphobics. Obviously, including patients without such symptoms was important in differentiating the personalities of phobic persons from others. As I will show in this book, people may have a phobic personality structure without showing anxiety symptoms. They may develop such symptoms later in specific situations in life, but some will remain without anxiety symptoms if they are never exposed to such situations.

In looking for personality traits associated with symptoms or syndromes one needs to see a large number of patients. If one observes certain personality traits in a patient with a particular symptom or set of symptoms, one cannot know whether the personality traits and the symptoms are in any way connected. They may occur jointly by chance. A knowledge of psychodynamics enables one to produce hypotheses that establish plausible connections. A hypothesis can, however, only be confirmed if a sufficient number of patients are examined.

The directing object

In his book on character and neurosis Hoffmann (1979) deplored the lack of a useful concept with which to address phobic personality structure. There are many forms of phobia but all phobic patients share a specific impairment in ego development concerning what I call the *internal directing object*. An internal directing object directs behaviour in accordance with social norms. The directing object is, normally, part of an internal object representation that develops from interactions with the mother or a mother substitute. Phobic patients look for *external* directing objects able to substitute for an internal directing object.

This shows in a patient's interactions with partners in private life, with colleagues at work, and with a therapist. The lack of a soundly functioning directing object does not have to result in phobic symptoms such as agoraphobia, animal phobia, or a fear of heights. It only results in phobic symptoms if a person is exposed to a specific trigger situation. The phobic personality structure develops during the period in which an obsessive-compulsive character structure may also be formed.

A mother may, for instance, prevent a child from learning by trial and error, out of a fear that this might result in accidents of all kinds. I term this behaviour type A (*anklammernd*, clinging). Another mother may behave in quite the opposite way: she may refrain from helping a child in his activities. I call this behaviour type D (distanced). Behaviour that helps a child to develop a soundly functioning internal directing object lies between the two extremes. A person's external directing objects may be of various kinds. Some adults take their mother as an external directing object and remain dependent on her. This often happens where the mother is of type A.

In people with a phobic personality structure, unconscious impulses to behave in a way that is not socially acceptable will approach consciousness but these impulses are warded off. The impulses are the cause of the anxiety, which is consciously experienced but is separated from the impulse that caused it. Anxiety is the main reason for avoidant behaviour in phobic people. In a way, this is the reverse of what we can observe in people with obsessive-compulsive character structures, who can experience the contents of the impulse but not the reasons for it. For example, an obsessive-compulsive mother may experience an impulse to hurt or even kill her child. Such a mother does not know *why* she might want to do this (isolation from context). The affect that causes the aggressive impulse is also kept unconscious (isolation from affect). In phobia, by contrast, the anxiety caused by an impulse becomes conscious while its contents, its context, and the accompanying fantasies all remain unconscious. Anxiety can trigger counterphobic behaviour, with a counterphobic person exposing himself to anxiety-causing situations. Avoiding these would cause a narcissistic injury.

As described above, in a normal development the directing object is part of an internal object representation that develops from interactions with the mother or mother substitute. Normally, the mother object is internalised. According to Schafer (1968), internalisation transforms real or fantasised regulating properties of an object into internal regulations. The internalisation of a directing object is based on a positively experienced relationship with the mother. The directing object is integrated into the self. If the relationship with the mother contains much aggression, the directing object may remain separated from the self representation: it is introjected but not integrated and in this way its competencies are not integrated either. The child will then look for external objects that can provide such competencies. Competencies may also be restricted if a child identifies with his mother's anxious reactions. The child will then refrain from acting in ways that produce these reactions.

The development and integration of a competent directing object can be negatively influenced by genetics. Thus, according to Kernberg (1975), excessive oral aggressiveness can be inherited, disturbing the development of a positive relationship with mother. The child projects his oral-aggressive self on to the mother, experiencing her as oral-aggressive. He will then react with anxiety or counter-aggression. Furthermore an oral-aggressive child will, in an average expectable environment (Hartmann, 1939), experience more oral frustrations than a child that is less oral-aggressive. Schultz-Hencke (1951) was another therapist who considered genetic factors to play an important role in psychic development and who referred to hyperactivity as a predisposition for obsessive-compulsive neurosis. The mother of a hyperactive child may react to his activity by restricting his freedom to move around. She may do this through aggressive actions such as scolding.

Contributing factors

Abraham (1914) supposed muscle contractions to produce erotic effects in some individuals, seeing these effects as fulfilling libidinal desires. He observed that agoraphobics who had been cured took pleasure in walking and physical exercise, and this was something they had much enjoyed before agoraphobia developed. One would assume that somebody whose movements had been restricted would enjoy moving when he could do so freely. This may be more important to people who are constitutionally predisposed to enjoy exercise.

Abraham also observed that people whose sexuality was restricted enjoyed exercise less than other people. For myself, I would assume that some patients whose sexuality is impaired may also feel depressed and for that reason refrain from taking much exercise.

As later described by Baumeyer (1950, 1959/1960), many agoraphobics have the desire to run away but this seems to have nothing to do with erotic feelings. Lopez-Ibor (1959) presupposes neurological factors in acrophobia but not in agoraphobia. Ficarra and Nelsen (1946/1947) found phobic symptoms, including agoraphobia, in hyperthyreotic patients, which disappeared when hyperthyreosis was successfully treated by somatic and by psychotherapeutic means. Hyperthyreosis is known to produce anxiety states, so it seems plausible that it may be an ancillary factor in the genesis of phobia.

The principal factor in the genesis of phobia, however, can be found in the interactions between the child and his mother or mother substitute. A mother may restrict learning by imitation, fearing that a child will run into danger if he imitates adults. For example, a child may want to cross a street, as he sees adults do, but without watching out for approaching traffic. Naturally, in some situations it will be the right thing to prevent a child from imitating adults, but a phobogenic mother may overreact and do so universally, showing anxiety any time a child imitates adults. This will have negative effects on the child's ability to learn by trial and error.

A child whose mother threatens to desert him may introject the mother object (Bowlby, 1970). In doing this the child is trying to mitigate the effects of being deserted. A mother's threat of leaving him may also cause a child to feel anger which may then be deflected on to the introject, and this can cause anxiety. Understanding these dynamics helps in understanding cardiac neurosis (see the section on cardiac neurosis, pp. 34–36). People with a poorly developed internal directing object also fear their drives *because they cannot deal with them competently*. Fantasies containing ideas of chaotically carrying out what a drive demands can stem from pre-oedipal and oedipal stages of development (Arlow, 1979). The intensity of drive-motivated desires, a person's competence in dealing with them, and factors related to the external world may all contribute to determining the intensity of anxiety experienced by a person in regard to drive-motivated fantasies.

In a person with an obsessive-compulsive personality structure we find complex configurations of defences adopted to deal with powerful impulses. The impulses may pass into consciousness but without an affect that could motivate the person to put them into practice. In other patients the impulse may come through and be acted on but without a context that might explain it. The causes of the impulse remains unconscious. Thus, in obsessive-compulsive people, impulses to act in a way that might prove dangerous in the light of former experiences are effectively warded off. In phobic people, whose parents have dealt with unwanted actions in a different and less punitive manner, impulses come nearer to consciousness, but their contents remain unconscious. Impulses trigger anxiety which enters consciousness and this makes phobics avoid situations in which such impulses may be triggered. When phobic patients are asked to talk about their very first memories of anything that has happened in their lives, they often describe some dramatic occurrence, such as falling from a tree or losing contact with mother in a crowd.

Obsessive-compulsive and phobic personality structures can coexist. They occur in those who, between two and four years of age, have experienced a combination of external influences leading to the development of both obsessive-compulsive and phobic character traits. This may happen if those caring for the child interact with him in two different styles (whether this is the mother in one style and the father in the other, or the two parents in one way as opposed to a nanny or child-minder in the other), the one style leading to the development of obsessive-compulsive character traits, the other to phobic character traits. It is also possible that one or both of the parents showed combinations of phobic and obsessive-compulsive personality structures.

If a mother (or a mother substitute) rarely interacts with the child, leaving him alone most of the time, the child will lack the opportunities to learn through having his actions accompanied by a discreetly supportive mother. When interacting with his mother, a young child may be close to her or later move away from her, learning to be by himself for a certain time and then returning to his mother for emotional refuelling (Mahler, Pine, & Bergman, 1975). If a mother, or mother substitute, expects the child to become as competent as one who is offered more opportunities to learn in interactions with his mother, this will also have negative effects on the child's self-esteem.

In an initial interview, a patient may not be able to remember much of what happened in the first three years of his life. (Even in analysis, he may never be able to remember much, or any, of this period, but the relationship with the mother will probably appear in the transference). However, in many cases, we will be able to extrapolate from descriptions of the mother when the patient was older.

This also holds true for patients without clinical phobic symptoms, who may have entered therapy for other reasons but who also show phobic character traits. They may never have been exposed to a specific triggering situation that could have caused phobic symptoms to appear. In some cases, a phobia may exist, but without manifest symptoms, because avoidance successfully prevents the development of anxiety.

A woman patient of mine entered analysis wishing to be cured of extreme jealousy. The jealousy was aroused by her dependence on her husband, whom she feared losing. He was an external directing object for her. The couple lived in a village near Göttingen and the patient felt safe in the village. It served as a directing object, due to the close social control that is often a feature of rural areas. She never came to Göttingen alone. She and her husband had only one car, so this seemed a reasonable solution but in fact, without her husband, the patient would have developed agoraphobic symptoms.

At a later stage, I shall show how my observations link up with previously existing concepts. In this chapter, I shall confine myself to describing the ideas of two authors on whom I have relied from the start (Müller-Braunschweig, 1970; Stierlin, 1971). Müller-Braunschweig mentions that a mother-introject cannot be integrated when there are strong aggressive affects in the relationship with the mother. Stierlin describes the *gyroscopic* functions of internal objects. Just as a gyroscope aids a ship in keeping to an intended direction, a gyroscopic internal object may direct a person to find a love object that is in some ways similar to an object in his inner world.

In the next section I shall describe my own views and point out the similarities and differences compared to Stierlin's views. In this context, I would like to mention that there may also be deficiencies in the development of a directing object in persons who have experienced traumatic influences in early object relations. In these cases, deficiencies in a directing object are part and parcel of a general, structural deficiency in the psyche and are linked to a general ego weakness, as in borderline syndromes described by Kernberg (1975).

The functions of internal and external objects

Stierlin (1971) gives the following definition: "An internal object determines the course a person will take in an interpersonal field, like a gyroscope which makes a ship go in a certain direction, compensating for the influence of weather conditions" (my translation). Thus, internal objects relating to the self can serve to choose external objects that are similar to them, such as choosing a partner who resembles the father or mother.

The directing object directs a person to behave in a competent manner in social situations. A person whose internal directing object does not function well will choose external objects that appear fitted to take on the role of an external directing object. This may combine with a tendency to look for partners that resemble a parent. However, a partner may be chosen even though he or she does not resemble a parent. In people who need an external directing object, the apparent capacity to serve as such an object takes priority in object choice. The chosen object may be an individual or it may be a group of people in an institution where the person works.

The choice of a directing object is not confined to humans. A dog may serve as a companion and be useful in preventing a person from moving about freely in a way he fears. For example, a woman taking a walk accompanied by her dog would be prevented, by the presence of the dog, from spontaneously following any invitation by a man to enter his house. Or a male patient with agoraphobia might feel safe walking in a street if he is pushing his bicycle, since before starting any kind of fight he would have to get rid of the bike and this would give him time to think (Streeck, 1978).

Stierlin describes how internal objects can function to foster autonomy. A person may engage in a kind of dialogue with his internal objects, thus making him less dependent on an external object. A similar idea was proposed by Kernberg (1975). A person can turn to his internal objects to ask what to do ("What would my mother or father say?"). He does not then need to consult actual people. This kind of inner dialogue may be prevented by aggressive feelings towards the internal object. According to Stierlin, the inner world is also a kind of container for expectations. The inner world can signal what to expect in a certain social situation and what may happen if you act in a certain way. Internal objects may leave a person little space for autonomous decisions; then what they seem to say becomes a command to be obeyed. Growing experience in the external world may then be unable to effect changes in a person's internal objects.

Thus, a person with internal objects of this kind cannot easily try out new ways of behaving in a particular situation. For example, an adult may feel obliged to act in the same way he did as a child, and may therefore not try out behaviour that would be better suited to an adult's social situation, with its new privileges and limitations.

By contrast, in a person whose internal objects allow themselves to be easily modified, these may have little power to determine how the person will act in the external world; they may leave a wide field of choices open but provide little guidance, for example, in the choice of partner. Stierlin in this context refers to Freud (1917) who stated that *identification* may be in the service of defence, but may also, in a normal development, serve to establish an individual identity. Balint (1956), Winnicott (1953, 1966) and Schafer (1968) see this in a similar way.

A relationship in which good feelings prevail is conducive to identification with the object. *Aggressive* feelings may lead to an introjection that then does not lead to identification. A hated introject may be experienced as necessary for survival and retain its influential status, or it may be isolated, as described by Müller-Braunschweig (1970). A mother may do the right things to foster the development of competence in a child. If, however, she is experienced as aggressive then a well-functioning internal directing object will not develop. The child will set up defences against the internal mother object. He may also choose a partner who appears to be the opposite of the hated parent.

We can make similar observations in the development of the superego. A superego may also be isolated if the internal objects from which it develops are experienced as very aggressive. Klüwer (1974) found evidence in antisocial adolescents of a sadistic superego that was, however, isolated by defences set up against it. In this way, these adolescents seemed to have no superego at all. In addition, an isolated superego may fail to be modified in the course of a person's development, remaining in an archaic state, and this keeps the defences against the superego active. (Therapies of antisocial patients often fail as a result of this).

Further remarks on the phobogenic mother
or mother substitute

In this section, I will reflect on the motives of a mother, or mother substitute, for behaving in a way that can lead to the development of a phobic personality structure in her child. A mother who fears that her child may run away or meet with an accident may be warding off aggressive impulses by reaction formation. In their wish to protect their children these mothers may anxiously overdo warning them of dangers, or they may impede any actions which might prove dangerous. The kind of initiatives that an average mother might see as signs of progress in her child's development, are met with anxiety. Seeing the child wanting to do something, such a mother, or mother substitute, will do it for him.

Later on, although a mother may want her adolescent daughter to become self-reliant, she may still take the job out of the girl's hands the moment she tries to do anything, perhaps claiming she is too slow, which may be true. If the girl has learned from her mother that anything she takes in hand may end in catastrophe, she may well become over-cautious. Another preconscious, or conscious, motive in a mother may be a wish, or a need, to keep the child dependent on her. Similarly, a son may be prevented from doing any work his mother can do for him. In this way, he remains dependent on his mother.

A mother's contribution to the development of a phobic personality structure starts when the very young child begins to move around, during the phase of separation-individuation. (Mahler, Pine, & Bergman, 1975). A mother of type A may be experienced by the child as intrusive, causing aggression, which may prevent identification with her. This aggression is usually warded off in an idealisation of the mother.

There are multiple reasons for type D behaviour. Often the mother has to work outside the home, or she wants to do so because she enjoys her job. A mother may consciously or unconsciously reject the child, or she may have a schizoid personality structure, remaining at a distance from most objects.

Narcissistic mothers may experience a child's lack of progress as humiliating to her; depressed mothers, or mothers who are not clinically depressed but have a depressive personality structure, may lack the will to initiate play with the child. They will blame themselves if the child does not progress as expected. When identification with the mother is difficult, a child will learn by imitation only. In some of these children the superego may substitute as a directing object.

In children with a type D mother we often see combinations of a phobic structure with a narcissistic, depressive, or schizoid one. Children whose mothers did not react with anxiety but rather with regulations and punishments, are more likely to develop an obsessive-compulsive personality structure. The children of mothers who threaten to desert them, or to become ill and perhaps die if the children do not do what their mothers want them to do, may develop cardiac neurosis.

The adaptive functions of anxiety

Unconscious signal anxiety (Freud, 1926) activates mechanisms of defence which protect the ego from being swamped by drives. These mechanisms also protect a person from committing actions that could cause guilt feelings, shame, or unwanted interpersonal reactions. Anna Freud (1936) describes various defence mechanisms to which a number were added later by various authors. Conscious anxiety without a conscious reason may be experienced when signal anxiety fails to trigger appropriate defence mechanisms. Signal anxiety is increased until it becomes conscious, breaking through the barrier between the preconscious and the conscious, this barrier being constituted by the second censor postulated by Sandler and Sandler (1994). The context in which signal anxiety was triggered does not become conscious.

Avoidance is, in a way, analogous to flight from a real or imagined danger. In phobias, however, the danger remains unconscious. Only anxiety becomes conscious and anxiety-provoking situations or objects are avoided. For example, an agoraphobic will stay away from the street, remaining in his house or flat. By contrast, one motive for exposing oneself to an anxiety-provoking situation may be the wish to avoid the humiliation which can be caused by anxiously staying away from it.

Phobic personality structures and symptoms

Also see Appendix.

Sigmund Freud (1908) was the first psychoanalyst to describe the character structure which we would now call the obsessive-compulsive personality. Psychiatric diagnostic manuals based on

ICD-10 (ICD, 2010) describe extreme personality structures requiring therapy. The same personality traits can be regarded as normal until they develop to a problematic extent. Western societies, highly differentiated in the realm of work, require a variety of personality structures. Whether or not a person is suited to do a certain job does not depend on talent alone. A bookkeeper needs to have a personality quite different from that of a person who works at the reception desk of a hotel, and surgeons will typically be different in their character structure from internists. We note also that the way a patient works in analysis or in analytic psychotherapy depends on the structure of his or her personality (König, 2001, 2004).

In the ICD-10 the phobic character structure described in this book is usually coded as a dependent personality disorder (a person with a phobic personality structure is dependent on his or her companion), or as an anxious personality disorder.

Psychoanalysts belonging to various schools of psychoanalysis (Fenichel, 1939, 1944, 1946; Fairbairn, 1952; Guntrip, 1961, 1968; Jacobson, 1971; Riemann, 1961) have used the categories of clinical personality structures in their clinical work with varying success. I myself have used a clinical typology based on Riemann (e.g., König, 1995a, 1995b, 2001, 2004, 2005, 2007, 2008, 2010, 2011) in a number of books in which I have attempted to show that a successful outcome of psychotherapy may depend on whether the working styles of patient and analyst are taken into account, starting with the choice of therapy. For example, patients with a depressive character structure will not do well in short-term therapy.

My observation of phobic personality structure began with a focus on agoraphobics, later on extended to patients with animal phobia, acrophobia, and, to a lesser extent, people with erythrophobia and other kinds of social phobia. I also paid particular attention to phobic character symptoms in patients who entered therapy without presenting anxiety symptoms. When I found phobic character traits, I enquired further into phobic symptoms. In many cases, the patients spoke of phobic symptoms such as animal phobia or acrophobia. They had not mentioned them before, because they did not consider them to be relevant, compared to the symptoms that had motivated them to enter therapy. However, not all patients with the specific traits of the phobic personality, mentioned phobic symptoms of any kind. Some patients, who had only recently developed phobic symptoms, described phobic traits which had been present before phobic symptoms appeared. This, by the way, shows that phobic personality traits are not by-products of a phobic symptomatology.

Some phobias persist from childhood, others appear for the first time when a person is exposed to a specific trigger situation. Others again are compensated for by specific arrangements that help to avoid triggering situations. I repeat: people with a phobic character structure are *disposed* to develop anxiety symptoms but they can be symptom-free, just as there are people with a depressive personality structure who are not depressed.

A phobic personality structure is rarely developed to the point of needing treatment in itself. However, as I shall be showing further on, it may impede a person's ability to work without a companion. In the presence of a companion, people with a phobic personality structure do not show much initiative but they often work to the satisfaction of their employers. In larger business organisations there is usually somebody higher up in the hierarchy who watches over and checks on a working person's performance.

More about the companion

A phobic person's companion substitutes for an insufficiently developed internal directing object. A "companion" can be a person, such as a partner in marriage, a friend, or a colleague, or it can be a group of people. An institution where the phobic person works can also function as a directing object. A phobic person can be happy to work in an institution where his ways of behaving are determined by the institution.

A person's relationship with a directing object is always ambivalent. The directing object is experienced as helping, but also as confining. The aggressive impulses forming part of this ambivalence are usually warded off. Thus, a phobic person rarely acts aggressively towards the directing object. Phobic people are often ambivalent about being promoted, since this might give them more leeway in the choice of ways in which they can act. This is also true for persons who consciously want to be promoted. Using rationalisations, they often find plausible reasons why promotion would not be appropriate for them. Of course, there are other reasons for avoiding promotion, for example, oedipal fantasies. A man may refuse promotion because he fears becoming stronger than the father figure and "killing" him.

The external directing objects need not always be higher in rank or stronger, nor need they be older than the phobic person. Except on his way to work, one agoraphobic patient was always accompanied when leaving the house by his child, who suffered from an inborn cardiac defect. He always took the same route, walking quickly and so reducing the danger of making contacts. When the boy got tired, which he soon did, the patient carried him. Later, an operation changed things: the child became able to run around freely, like any healthy boy of his age, upon which the father developed agoraphobic symptoms.

The accompanying object does not have to be a person. This was reported by Westphal (1872), and later by Marks (1970). One of my patients, a policeman, was able to move about freely when in uniform. His uniform made him behave as a policeman has to: he knows he is not allowed to drink alcohol in a pub, or strike up an informal conversation with just anyone he finds interesting, and he is not allowed to use force except when this can be justified. Without his uniform this policeman showed agoraphobic symptoms. In another case (Streeck, 1978) an inanimate object served as a companion. After several years of analysis, a young schoolteacher had almost entirely lost his agoraphobic symptoms but slight anxiety remained when he walked along a street. He did not, however, experience any anxiety when he was pushing a bicycle. He could not just let the bicycle drop to the ground in order to follow an impulse; he knew he had to dispose of it, for example, by leaning it up against a wall, which would have given him time to think. This was sufficient to prevent anxiety.

Many agoraphobic patients often tell us that they do not experience anxiety when driving (Marks, 1970), while others, fearing to cause an accident, do experience anxiety. Those who do not experience anxiety use the car like a house where they can feel safe. When they develop anxiety in the street they retreat into their car, which isolates them from people outside.

The phobic working style

Phobic people often have little confidence in their ability to do good work. During their childhood, doing things themselves met with anxious reactions from their mothers. Often mother, or a mother substitute, meaning to be helpful, will herself have done what the child was trying to accomplish. A mother, or mother substitute, may, on the other hand, neglect to provide opportunities for learning. Instead of helping when necessary she may not help at all but expect the child to make as much progress as one who is being supported in his endeavours, receiving help when it is needed. In both cases, children will not learn enough and will not develop the self-confidence to expect to succeed in what they are doing, or at least expect to be able to learn. Right from the start a phobic person will not expect to do things well, and this will also concern things he has in fact done before in the past. The impulse to do something is accompanied by an anxiety signal which motivates the phobic person to procrastinate. There is a German saying, meant as a joke, which can aptly be applied to phobics: "If you feel an urge to do some work, just sit down quietly somewhere and let it pass".

In a patient, disorders of this kind in attitudes to work can, in many cases, only be recognised on the basis of painstaking diagnostic work. The behaviour of a phobic person resembles that of a depressive, who lacks initiative, experiences no urge to act, and who can only work if he is forced to do so. Phobic people may feel an impulse to act but this impulse is accompanied by an anxiety signal. Often, they do not even notice an impulse, they only feel the anxiety. Some phobic patients may say that the work they are expected to do is boring, or does not make sense, or use some other kind of rationalisation. Other phobics may not be able to use a telephone because this would mean exposing themselves to the outside world without any visual feedback to guide them. They use other ways of communicating and avoid jobs that demand the use of a telephone.

People with a depressive structure often feel they must do a certain kind of work *very well*. Phobics, by contrast, feel they cannot do a certain kind of work even with *average results*. Thus, a phobic university student, who had taken his bicycle apart in order to clean it, could not put it back together, but he was able to do so when a friend came by and just stood there watching him, without participating in the work or telling him how to do it. Phobic disorders over work are easier to treat than depressive ones, since the impulse to do something is not totally blocked.

Phobic performers, who have to present themselves before an audience, often experience stage fright. They may have performed well in rehearsals, with nobody watching them, but they experience stage fright when the curtain goes up and all eyes are upon them. The audience is experienced as a mother object (König, 1976) who will judge the performer and find him wanting. A performer will often lose his anxiety with the first applause, as this is interpreted as showing the mother's approval. In this context, it is interesting to note that Greenson (1967), in his textbook on psychoanalytic therapy, mentions that analysts often suffer from stage fright, (for example, when reading a paper at a conference). An analyst does his daily work without an audience. As the patient is the only person listening to him, there is no occasion to follow any exhibitionistic impulse, which would consciously, and often to a greater degree unconsciously, be experienced as dangerous. In classical analysis, with the patient on a couch, it is the patient who is expected to take the initiative, thus determining the subject of the session. The analyst follows the patient, as it were. Analysts can experience the patient as directing them, and when they offer an interpretation, validation is left to the patient.

To take a simple example of a piece of work: writing a letter. Every professional who has worked in a hospital will have met the difficulty of writing letters to describe diagnoses and treatments and to propose next steps. It is natural to put off such tasks, but procrastinating over the writing of such letters may be based on various different disorders. As mentioned before, depressive working disorders have something to do with a lack of initiative, sometimes, also, with a perfectionistic attitude. An obsessive-compulsive attitude, too, can lead to a perfectionistic working style. A perfect letter for an obsessive-compulsive person has to be *comprehensive*. An obsessive-compulsive often finds it difficult to select what is really important, causing the recipient of his letter to drown in details. Narcissistic people want to prove that they can write very good letters but fear to prove themselves wrong in this. People with a hysterical or histrionic character structure often strongly dislike paper work, especially when precise information is expected. People with a phobic character structure feel anxiety about giving information without receiving any direct feedback. This anxiety is similar to the anxiety felt when using a telephone.

People with a phobic personality structure do not want to carry the final responsibility for work; they feel more comfortable just assisting. Since they are often popular with their superiors, phobics may be chosen for a post with considerable responsibility. They can function well in this position if they have staff they can use as directing objects. Difficulties arise when there is not enough time to consult their staff.

Phobic colleagues may use the boss as a directing object. This can work quite well but they may run into difficulties if the aggressive part of their ambivalence towards the directing object becomes conscious, as it often does in therapy. Counterphobic heads of a business often over-tax their teams. They want them to show courage and independence. In this they act like type D mothers, expecting rapid progress on a job without their team requiring pointers and help.

A phobic person's partner choices

Partner choice in phobics is determined to a great extent by whether a prospective partner seems suited to take on the role of a phobic's companion. This is a reason why the successful therapy of a phobic patient may lead to separation from his partner, who was chosen for this suitability, other criteria having receded into the background. A companion can make an agoraphobic patient appear non-symptomatic. For example, I once knew a university professor who could only write papers when his wife was present. It was not that she was in a position to help him directly with his work; her mere presence was sufficient.

As mentioned before, the relationship with a companion is always ambivalent, aggressive elements being warded off. This defence may consist of suppression, repression, or idealisation. In the relationship with mother, the aggressive component of ambivalence is quite often warded off through idealisation. Indeed, when a patient describes his mother as an ideal person, a therapist should always think of this as a defence against the aggressive part of ambivalence and perhaps be awake to a possible phobic personality structure. (There are, of course, other reasons for defensive idealisation.) In relations with a partner, too, aggression may also be repelled through idealisation. A patient of mine said: "I can speak French and I play the piano. My husband can cook better than I do. It is not necessary to play the piano. There are very few occasions when I have an opportunity to speak French. Cooking has to be done every day. My husband can do anything or learn how to do it. I can do practically nothing".

Phobics frequently mention reliability as the most important criterion in their choice of partner. Often, obsessive-compulsive partners are chosen. In this, phobics resemble histrionics. Histrionic people admire systematic thinking and rational behaviour in complex situations. They often make a complementary choice, choosing a partner who seems to have what they lack; they are inclined to behave in a chaotic manner. Phobics do not behave this way, but they unconsciously fear it might happen; so they look for an orderly and reliable partner. Phobics may also choose other phobics. The partners are then companions for each other (Kreische, 2004). In a case described by Kreische, one partner took a counterphobic role, and used his partner to stabilise him in his counterphobic position. He postponed a necessary operation he was afraid of, saying, and indeed believing, that he must care for his wife, who suffered from cardiac neurosis. Phobics are little inclined to end a partnership, so in a "phobic to phobic" relationship both partners can to a large extent rely on staying together. Some phobics choose a partner who reminds them of the mother who belittled and criticised them. Others choose partners who remind them of their mothers in some other way. As defensive idealisation of the partner diminishes in the course of therapy, aggression comes to the foreground. Therapy of the partner may help him to stay, if the relationship can develop beyond the phobic arrangement.

It can also happen that obsessive-compulsive companions, whether male or female, enjoy helping their partner, because this puts them in a superior position, and they may not like the phobic partner to become more self-reliant and thus no longer need their help. A depressively structured companion may see the partner's aggressions as justified, since these tally with his low self-esteem. Schizoid persons do not, as a rule, accept the role of a phobic's companion. They do not like living with someone for whom it is important to remain in constant contact. There are, however, some phobics who are content with little contact, but they want the companion to remain permanently available. This often happens if phobics have a depressive streak, which makes them feel they do not deserve a better deal.

Phobics with cardiac neurosis usually cling to a partner. For them, the companion represents their mother and their mother is equated with their heart. Losing the companion would mean losing the mother in her internal representation, located in the heart.

Men with a phallic-narcissistic personality structure may behave like strong and reliable people and so be chosen as a companion by the phobic. They are, however, fundamentally unsure of their male identity so they overreact to criticism of their masculinity. In the long run this makes them unreliable, because the slightest criticism can activate doubts of their being the strong and competent man they wish to be. They may react to criticism with aggression or with panic.

People with a histrionic personality structure are rarely chosen as companions to phobics. They lack reliability. Some people with a character structure of this type will be able to behave as desired by their phobic partner for a while but they cannot keep it up for long.

A phobic person's travelling style

One of the impulses fended off by persons with a phobic personality is the impulse simply to run away (Baumeyer, 1950) without a clear destination or without previous planning. A phobic patient experienced her first anxiety attack while sitting in a railway station restaurant, waiting for a train which was to carry her to a place inside Germany, when suddenly a train to Milan, was announced over the loudspeaker system. The announcement triggered in her an impulse to run away from her present life situation, perhaps to a place outside Germany, like Milan in Italy, by boarding this train.

Agoraphobics often want to travel to faraway places and to do so without a companion. They do not like their constrained way of life, being dependent on a companion, and they develop the notion that in faraway, exotic places life would be different and their present troubles would disappear. One agoraphobic patient was unable to walk around in the streets of the town where she lived. She would run to her car, which she used when visiting friends. On arriving at their house, she would park the car and then run into the house. On the other hand, she was well able to travel to countries such as Egypt and Morocco, where her agoraphobic symptoms were no longer active, and where she was able to move around freely.

This may sound surprising. It seems to have something to do with the fact that in such countries, foreign tourists are not expected to behave the way the natives do. If you make mistakes, you can point out you are a foreigner, that you do not speak the language, and are not acquainted with local customs. Also, the police are usually instructed to help foreign tourists and contact with people is restricted and ritualised, for example, in a hotel, a restaurant, or on guided tours.

In another example of agoraphobic choice, the French Foreign Legion provides a setting offering strict discipline in a clear hierarchical structure, combined with opportunities to visit foreign countries and move around them in uniform, the uniform imposing a certain kind of behaviour. I remember two Germans who had served in the French Foreign Legion. Both were agoraphobics. The impulses which were warded off were running away, latent homosexuality, and aggressiveness. In the Foreign Legion the men could travel to foreign countries where they had to behave in a certain way, they could act aggressively in harmony with their military role, and homosexual acts were prohibited.

Some agoraphobics of the counterphobic variety experience foreign countries in a different way: as places of adventure, posing challenges they can take up. This can help them overcome their agoraphobic anxiety. At the same time, they liberate themselves from their mothers' efforts to keep them tied to home, forbidding them to leave the house or garden connected to the house. Phobic men who travel alone in foreign countries may feel free to have sexual intercourse there since they can imagine that no long-lasting relationship is intended by their sexual partner. They usually live in long-term relationships with a companion in their own country, where the mere fantasy of starting a sexual relationship with another woman would cause intense anxiety. They feel that short-term sexual relationships in a foreign country will not endanger the relationship with the partner at home, who functions as a companion.

Comparison with antisocial personality structure

Patients with antisocial personality structures (Kernberg, 1975) do what phobic people fear to do. Their directing object is often underdeveloped. They do not develop defences against impulses that result in antisocial behaviour. One could say that they do not feel a necessity to do so. People with an antisocial personality structure often seem to have no superego. During therapy, when defences are weakened, phobic patients often develop fantasies about becoming antisocial, or they imagine, or in fact go through, a period of behaving in a way that could be called antisocial. One married phobic patient who worked in a university, but also did a great deal of work at home, and who lived with his family in a three-room flat, had an idea of renting a room in another building in order to be able to work undisturbed. He did not actually do so because of a fantasy of losing control of himself and of spending his days and evenings drinking, taking up a relationship with another woman, or leaving for Africa.

Another phobic patient spent some vacations in Greece at a time in the analysis when her defences against impulses had weakened their hold. She once played a prank, moving around certain objects on the altar of a Greek orthodox church and changing the places where the robes of the priests and the altar boys were hung. This caused considerable confusion before and during the next service, as she learned from people who had attended it. The patient came from a very pious family.

CHAPTER ONE

Psychoanalysis of phobia

Making the first contact

When meeting a phobic patient for the first time, a therapist may observe specific ways of behaving. Some phobics will talk a lot. There are different ways of doing this: an "anal" flow of words is usually experienced as aggressive and overwhelming and will cause irritation in a listener, while an "urethral", perhaps elegant, flow of words may, if well executed, cause envy or feelings of rivalry, but it may also make a listener depreciate the content of what is being said. By contrast, a phobic's flow of words is often experienced as interesting and pleasant. It makes for easy listening. However, a psychotherapist may find that she is being kept at a distance, making it difficult to get a word in. A phobic flow of words also seems to retain the listener, keeping her from leaving. This corresponds to what a child may have wanted to achieve: namely to keep his mother at a certain distance without losing contact, which would be the case of a child with a restrictive mother or with a mother who demanded more than the child was capable of. Such behaviour in a patient may irritate the therapist, since she may thus be prevented from asking for specific information, or from confronting the patient when he is circumventing particular topics.

Phobics have often learnt how to make people like them and feel obliged to help them. When a phobic patient enters the consulting room, he may—with slight, discreet signals—cause the therapist to do things she would not otherwise do. The therapist may then fell the need to direct the patient to the seat provided for patients, explaining the seating arrangement, perhaps explaining what she wants to find out, instead of just letting things develop. The little details involved in this first contact can be most revealing. For instance, one consulting room in a house where I received patients in my private practice, had a double door. The outer door had a magnet which kept it closed. You could open it in the way you might open the door of a fridge. When patients came for a first consultation, I would receive them at the door of the house and accompany them to my consulting room. When a patient left, I would take leave in the consulting room and open the inner door. Most patients, who did not have a phobic personality structure, would try to turn the knob on the outer door and, when they noticed that it could not be turned, would push it open. Phobic patients, after trying to turn the door knob, stopped and looked back at me for instructions. Patients with social phobia only behaved like this if the phobic part of the personality was stronger than the narcissistic part, which is usually the case in social phobias. Counterphobic patients they just pushed. And finally, according to Richter and Beckmann (1969), patients with cardiac neurosis type A, who are very dependent on parental figures, produced very strong signals. They suddenly looked anxious and in urgent need of help.

A phobic patient in classical psychoanalysis

The analyst sitting behind a phobic patient who is lying on a couch will comment on what the patient is saying or keeping back. The patient may experience this as being similar to what he experienced during childhood. The analyst pays attention to what a patient is doing or not doing, like the mother of a toddler who is quietly attentive to the child in his endeavours. The analyst may do this in different ways, according to how she experiences the relationship with the patient at any given moment. When an analyst addresses conflicts, a patient may assume that he is being criticised for not doing things in the right way, for not being able to do what is expected or for not wanting to do so. Thus the patient may experience the analyst's activities as a repetition of the childhood experience of being criticised by the mother for ineptitude, which can lead to the failure of an analysis if the analyst does not bring this up for discussion and reflection.

The phobic patient feels very dependent on the analyst, at least as long as aggressive and distancing impulses do not reach consciousness. Protests over the behaviour of the analyst in dealing with the patient will not at first be consciously experienced but unconscious protest may prevent the patient from accepting interpretations and using them productively. If an analyst takes into account what effect the psycho-analytic setting itself can have on a phobic patient, she can interpret this and thus prevent the analysis from becoming unproductive.

Most phobics have negative opinions of themselves with regard to what they are capable of doing but, whereas a depressive patient will feel "no good" or worthless based on the experience of never having been nursed or fed in a caring way as a very young child, a phobic patient will have developed a negative self-image because he was made to feel incapable of competent behaviour. In addition, phobic people have not previously had sufficient opportunities to learn by trial and error. This results in a real lack of competence, which is a fact that has to be addressed and worked through.

Phobic patients often induce an analyst to treat them with special care and caution and to demand less of them than they can, in fact, handle or tolerate. They have learned to convince others that they should not demand too much of them, since they are very sensitive and ought to be protected from all kinds of demands. This often shows on first contact with them. If the analyst does not confront this in time then long and unproductive analyses may result.

Phobic patients may have learned to motivate other people to do things for them. For example, they will not finish a sentence, leaving it to somebody else to complete it, or when they feel confused about a particular subject they simply wait for clarification, or they confine themselves to hints instead of saying clearly what they want to com-municate. They can manage to make the analyst complete their sen-tences for them, clarify confused communications, or interpret what their hints may mean. In this way a situation from their childhood is repeated. Like the mother, the analyst takes things in hand and acts in place of the patient. To a certain extent it may be necessary to do this at the beginning of the therapy, but with due caution and restraint, since an overdose of this behaviour will prevent change. For many phobic patients free association is difficult. "Moving around" in their own psyche without knowing what they, or what the analyst, may discover is not something they wish to do. Some patients just keep repeating similar ideas, regardless of what they are free-associating to. They remain, so to speak, within an area they know well. When they reach the borders of the territory they are already familiar with, free association comes to a halt. One patient, at this point, always said: "Today I can't find anything new". Many phobic patients do not free-associate to dreams or dream elements, thus preventing the latent contents of the dream from being linked to consciousness and to everyday life. Some leave it to the analyst to take the last few steps. They want the analyst to take responsibility for the contents of the dream as regards any influence it may have on the patient's future actions. Infantile impulses of which the patient is afraid may lose some of their anxiety-provoking potential if they are described by the analyst. This is part of the work of containing in every analysis, but phobic patients may want more of it than others do.

Those phobic patients whose mothers have behaved intrusively may reject every "move" on the analyst's part. This kind of resistance can be very difficult to dissolve. To succeed, the analyst needs to confront it directly, taking great care to let the patient know that the analyst understands and accepts the fact that the patient needs to show this resistance at the present stage of treatment (and mentioning that this may become unnecessary in the future). The flow of speech characteristic of phobic people often ceases when the patient lies down on the couch, begins to lack orientation, and therefore feels in danger. Patients then try, either verbally or by remaining silent, to make the analyst take the active part, in order to gain more orientation.

Analysts with a phobic personality structure

As mentioned before, an analyst in his consulting room is separated from the outer world. Since most analysts sit behind the patient, the visual contact between patient and analyst is avoided. To a certain extent, this protects the analyst from allowing exhibitionistic tendencies exert an influence. Greenson (1967) mentions that many analysts tend to suffer from "stage fright" and are relieved when they can take a seat behind the patient. The analyst's professional role can serve as a directing object. The analyst follows the patient, who is supposed to start speaking and thus initiate a theme which will determine the direction that work may take in the session. Kohut (1977) suggests that one of the reasons why Freud chose the now classic setting was that he had not been able to work through some exhibitionistic tendencies in his self-analysis. This cannot, of course, be used as an argument against the classic setting. The personal reasons Freud may have had for creating it do not detract from the value of the analytic setting itself. After all, Columbus' discovery of America was no less an historic achievement because he had, in fact, set out to find a sea route to India.

The fact that an analyst has a phobic personality structure does not predetermine her to be manipulated by the patient into behaving like a phobic's mother. However, a phobic disposition in the analyst may make it easier for a phobic patient to manipulate her, and the analyst may, as a result, wish to retain a patient longer than necessary, or become anxious when the patient wants to choose his own way. In Freud's time, patients were often asked not to take decisions of central importance in their lives while in analysis. Analyses did not last as long as they do in our day. Nowadays most analysts ask the patient to bring up any such decisions in analysis. An anxious analyst may then prevent a patient from taking a decision at all, keeping the patient from taking this step until it is no longer possible, because the situation has by then changed.

An analyst in the position of a phobic mother may carry out tasks that properly belong to the patient. On the other hand, if the analyst has slipped into the role of the phobic child—a position often taken by analysts who have a phobic personality structure—she may do quite the opposite and show reluctance to take on the analytical work required. This can lead some analysts to overemphasise the importance of free association and be unwilling to interrupt it by interpreting the material a patient brings up, with the result that this material may remain unused.

An analyst with phobic traits may ward them off with counterphobic behaviour and will then tend to be very active, overtaxing the patient and directly or indirectly asking him to take risks. This in a way resembles the behaviour of the distancing mother (type D), and shows an expectation of behaviour that the patient has not yet had the opportunity to become familiar with and to learn. In cases where the patient describes his mother as clinging (type A), analysts may try to behave differently from this type. They then find themselves falling into the pattern of counterphobic behaviour described above and, therefore, also overtaxing the patient. Equally, analysts who are trying hard to avoid behaving like a type D mother may fall into the trap of behaving in an intrusive manner. This can cause the patient to resist the analyst's efforts.

Phobic analysts observe a patient keenly in order to keep the relationship stable and harmonious. They may then limit themselves to doing what the patient will like. This can lead to an avoidance of necessary confrontations or of interpretations that a patient will not like, since they cause anxiety, shame, or guilt. As in all fields of work, a phobic person in the working role of an analyst may lack initiative. Initiative is not blocked, as it is in depressive people, but it causes anxiety and may therefore be avoided. Some phobic analysts limit themselves to non-verbal interventions, such as "hmm", to show that they are listening, and not do much else.

Counterphobic analysts may want patients to find things out by themselves, when they are not yet able to do so, whereas phobic analysts often use too much clarification, explaining to their patients what they mean by an interpretation, although the patients could find this out by themselves. In this respect, counterphobic therapists may explain too little. Phobic analysts may behave in an anxiously protective way, trying to prevent the patient from acting dangerously outside the session, while counterphobic therapists may provoke risk-taking behaviour in a patient, often by their tone of voice or by non-verbal interventions such as "hmm".

Projective identification can make phobic therapists allow themselves to be projectively identified with good objects but not so readily with bad ones. In this respect they resemble a depressive therapist. Counterphobic therapists can resist identification with a helping object, preventing themselves from helping even when offering help is indicated. In phobic therapists, resistance on the part of a patient is usually met with patience. Longer than others, phobic therapists may try to understand why a patient resists, and will hesitate to confront resistance, thinking that the patients may still need their resistance. This can be useful but it can also make a therapy take longer than necessary. A counterphobic therapist may tackle a resistance head on, thereby making it increase.

Working through takes place both inside and outside the session (Greenson, 1967). During the session, phobic therapists may take more time for working through, since they want to make sure that the patient has been sufficiently prepared. Outside the session, phobic therapists expect a patient to move cautiously, not risking too much and taking the needs and wishes of people he deals with well into account. Counterphobic therapists do the reverse, wanting their patients to take risks, and this may lead to discouraging failures.

Phobic therapists like a patient to report on what he has done and experienced outside the session. They usually work less in the here and now than others, preferring to work on the relationships a patient has outside the analytic dyad, keeping conflicts out of the analytic relationship. They want to help a patient to deal with *external* interpersonal conflicts. Counterphobic therapists work more in the here and now than phobic therapists, but they may overtax patients in expecting them to tolerate conflicts with the therapist when they are not yet able to do this. Some phobic therapists may prevent a patient from learning by trial and error, just as phobic mothers of type A do. In a way, they would prefer to accompany patients in their lives outside the session, watching over them and helping them when they do something risky. Counterphobic therapists will want patients to rely on themselves.

In deciding whether to take on a patient or not, phobic therapists may wonder whether a patient will accept them as a directing object or rather take this role himself. Some patients will show reasonable self-reliance and competence and so seem suitable to take a companion's role, doing much of the work themselves, and not overtaxing the directing capacity of the therapist. The phobic therapist may then prefer a patient of this kind to one who requires more help. Counterphobic therapists will act in a similar fashion, requiring, however, courage and self-reliance more than competence. This may lead to their choosing a type of therapy that overtaxes the patient.

Phobic therapists often adapt more than others to what they feel a patient wants or needs. This can prove useful. However, this may also make them avoid confronting the patient when it is necessary. When a phobic therapist has taken the patient as a directing object, the therapist remains passive while the patient is active. This may be a sensible thing to do, but it may also be done in the service of avoidance.

In summary, some phobic therapists seem to avoid all interventions that could make the patient angry. Counterphobic therapists, by contrast, risk interventions that prove "too much" for the patient, too much to tolerate. They also expect their patients to take risks in their daily lives. This may at times be useful, but if a patient fails in some undertaking, this can cause him to lose the self-confidence which is necessary to make further progress.

A phobic therapist in the role of a directing object may want to give more directions as to the patient's behaviour outside the session than the patient can take. During the hour, she may give long explanations. In this, she resembles obsessive-compulsive therapists, but the motives are different. Obsessive-compulsive therapists want their patients to behave in the way the therapist considers to be right. A phobic therapist wants to prevent the patient from suffering "accidents" in the area of social relationships.

Confronting patients, as conceptualised by Greenson (1967), means asking them to turn their attention to certain aspects of what they have said or done, or avoided saying and doing. In confronting a patient, the therapist takes the lead. A phobic therapist may want to avoid this and, by avoiding confrontation, may by-pass important material, whereas a counterphobic therapist is likely to employ risky confrontations that traumatise the patient or increase resistance.

In offering an interpretation a therapist takes responsibility, establishing links the patient has not thought of before. Phobic patients often want the therapist to do this. A phobic therapist may feel anxious when taking this responsibility. A phobic therapist may also try to ignore a patient's aggressiveness, instead of confronting it, or may interpret it very early on, thus preventing it from reaching the level of intensity needed for an interpretation to produce change.

To sum up: a phobic therapist will avoid taking the lead, confronting a patient, or naming links a patient may not like to learn about, while a counterphobic therapist may be too active, overcompensating for her own latent or manifest anxiousness.

CHAPTER TWO

Various types of phobia

In this part of the book I wish to compare what I have presented so far to what other authors have had to say about various types of phobia. I shall start with agoraphobia, because of its clinical and theoretical relevance. Then I turn to the role of a companion, which I would call an external directing object and which I first mentioned in papers on agoraphobia in various different theoretical contexts. I shall then discuss claustrophobia, animal phobia, school phobia, acrophobia, and cardiac neurosis.

Agoraphobia

What is warded off in agoraphobia?

Most authors mention libidinous and aggressive impulses stemming from the oedipal phase of development. Thus, Abraham (1913, 1914, 1921, 1922), Helene Deutsch (1928), Alexander (1930), and Bergler (1951), as well as Freud himself (1926) interpret the street as a place where a person may meet sexual temptation. Deutsch also takes aggressive, exhibitionistic, or scoptophilic impulses into consideration, as does Fenichel (1946). Anny Katan-Angel (1937) takes street traffic as a symbol for parental sexual intercourse, mobilising scoptophilic impulses. Abraham (1914) supposes that walking can be eroticised, at least in some people, depending on their constitution. Kuiper (1973) sees a woman's fantasy of prostituting herself as occurring in women of the revenge type described by Abraham (1921), who considers a woman's prostituting herself to be an aggressive act, since the prostitute does not really give to men what they want. Anny Katan-Angel (1937) sees agoraphobia in real prostitutes as the result of a displacement of a daughter–father relationship on to the men they may meet in the street. This incestuous fantasy she sees as more anxiety-provoking than actually sleeping with strangers. Miller (1953) describes a combination of several phantasies defensively warded off in the analysis of one patient.

Baumeyer (1959/60) examined 100 patients. In seventy patients he found a tendency to run away. He describes a conflict between a wish for freedom of movement and the wish to remain in safety. The wish to run away may mean running away from an intolerable life situation, to a place where a better life is possible. Gebsattel (1959) also addresses agoraphobia as relating to a child–mother relationship that provided little freedom of movement. In his view, agoraphobics may want to run away in order to look for a better mother. Some agoraphobics he examined had lived the life of a tramp but developed agoraphobia when they began to stay in one place and running away would have had bad consequences. Some authors, including Gebsattel, consider that open squares in a town suggest a free choice of direction which triggers anxiety, while others (like Marks, 1970) see them as locations that provide an opportunity to meet people. Possibly there are two kinds of agoraphobics: some fear meeting people who tempt them to transform sexual or aggressive fantasies into action; others wish to run away from their present life situation, as they may have wished to leave a confining and restricting mother. Running away would, however, result in negative social or economic consequences.

A restricting life situation also provides protection from behaving in an uncontrolled manner, which might lead to social disapproval. Being accompanied by another person may restrict possibilities of moving in all directions, since choosing a certain direction must be approved, or at least tolerated, by the companion. The companion may also prevent contact with strangers, who might tempt the agoraphobic to do something he is unconsciously afraid of doing.

The role of the ego

Until the second half of last century, analysts seemed to have accepted Freud's concept (Freud, 1926) of the displacement of an internal conflict on to the outer world, thereby transforming an internal danger into an external one, which can then be avoided by staying at home, for example. In agoraphobia, displacement may cause a street to symbolise, or make a person think of, prostitution.

However, being in a street can also provide real opportunities of making contact, which might lead to sexual intercourse. The street is thus a place which can tempt a woman to act in a way that she defensively wards off. In males, the temptation might rather be to get into a fight. I remember a professional football player who had to stop playing football because of an injury he had suffered on the football field. The game had offered him the opportunity to channel his aggression and on losing this he developed agoraphobia.

Freud's concepts of symbolisation and displacement seemed plausible and sufficient to explain agoraphobia. When repression fails, other means of defence are needed. When repression succeeds, instinctual impulses remain confined to the unconscious. Repression may fail because impulses to act are too powerful or the ego is too weak to suppress them. Later on, Weiss (1935, 1953, 1957, 1964, 1966), who applies Federn's (1956) ideas about ego weakness, supposes that in some patients, libidinal energy has been withdrawn from parts of the ego, resulting in a weakness of the ego. Anna Freud (1977) observes external triggers to increase existing anxiety in children, at times to a level of panic. Then externalisation on to a symbol which can be avoided may occur. However, she mentions that whether or not symbolisation is possible depends on the state of ego development. In our day, it seems to be generally accepted that an ego structured like that of a very young child may partly persist in adults. This may, for example, happen when ego development has not been sufficiently stimulated or not supported in a helpful way by interactions with objects in the outside world.

According to Fenichel (1944), anxiety has something to do with the ego not being able to deal with external reality, following the reality principle. This tallies with the real lack of competencies found in patients with agoraphobia. In addition, phobic persons underestimate the competencies they do have. According to Fenichel, when the ego is swamped by instinctual impulses that it cannot deal with rationally, a state of excitement is produced that may be unbearable. Today, Fenichel's ideas certainly apply to adults with a borderline pathology who may also produce phobic, at times agoraphobic, symptoms.

Weiss (1935, 1953, 1957, 1964, 1966), who was in analysis with Federn, adopts his descriptions of what the ego can or cannot do (Federn, 1956). He accepts Federn's hypotheses concerning ego weakness. As mentioned above, Federn explains this as being due to a deficit in libidinal energy.

To sum this up: Federn and Weiss do not use concepts which link anxiety to arrested ego development. They see a lack of instinctual energy invested in the ego as the cause of ego weakness in agoraphobia, whereas I consider the cause to be the lack of a well-integrated directing object due to specific kinds of interaction with the mother or mother substitute, or generally to a lack of interaction with others. The result is that an internal directing object is not sufficiently developed.

In the classical oedipal situation, a child may perhaps generate fantasies of some kind of sexual relationship with a parent, but normally father or mother do not participate and such fantasies are not transformed into real interactions. An adult allowing his behaviour to be determined by oedipal fantasies can experience aggressive impulses towards a person his partner relates to. This can lead to acts that prove destructive and, in consequence, self-destructive. Any prospect of acting like this may cause preconscious anxiety that becomes conscious if the person's mechanisms of defence are not activated or, if activated, are not strong enough to keep the anxiety caused by an antisocial impulse unconscious. The impulse itself is kept unconscious. Thus, an agoraphobic woman may feel tempted by people she meets in the street, especially if they remind her of her father, and may feel anxiety without knowing its context.

The companion as seen by Weiss (1957) substitutes for a part of the body experienced as deficient or lacking, such as the penis. Weiss sees the agoraphobic's companion as a kind of prosthesis completing his ego and resulting in the agoraphobic's ability to function better than he could without it. In my opinion, the companion serves to substitute for a deficiency in a part of the ego, which is linked to ego functions and prevents antisocial acts. Weiss, in describing agoraphobics, reports them as experiencing a lack of the energy needed to deal with certain situations in real life. Here, in my view, this behaviour is caused by a real lack of competence and by unrealistically low self-esteem with regard to the competencies the phobic person does have.

According to Weiss, leaving a house to go into the street may make agoraphobics feel they are leaving part of their ego behind. Patients who experience anxiety in their own house or flat can be helped by a companion. Weiss sees a companion as being able to substitute for a deficient part of the ego (*verstümmeltes Ich*, mutilated ego). This comes close to my idea of an ego which lacks something, namely a well-functioning internal directing object. The difference between our conceptions lies in the idea of how a deficient ego comes to develop. In my opinion, the ego itself is deficient, while Weiss seems to see the libidinal energy as being withdrawn from an otherwise normal part of the ego. In my view it is, as it were, rather more of a hardware problem, whereas Weiss perceived it as one of software.

Weiss observes that phobic people, having lost a partner who has functioned as a companion, may regress and return to their mother to find a relationship that completes them. Weiss takes a wish to feel whole as motivating a return to the mother: the feeling of wholeness was lost when the companion was lost. In my opinion, returning to a mother object after having lost a partner represents returning to the first external directing object.

Depersonalisation and derealisation in agoraphobia

Both these defence mechanisms are frequently found in agoraphobics. Roth (1959) examined 135 patients who showed depersonalisation and derealisation along with phobic symptoms. Derealisation and depersonalisation were not always present at the same time. Roth called a combination of the two, phobic-anxiety-depersonalisation-syndrome. The patients showed signs of psychic developmental arrest. Roth primarily considered somatic reasons such as occur in temporal lobe epilepsy. As early as 1928 Helene Deutsch described characteristics of anxiety attacks which one could ascribe to depersonalisation or derealisation.

Nunberg (1932) considers depersonalisation to be caused by a split in the ego produced by instinctual dynamics, as do Bergler and Eidelberg (1935) and Oberndorf (1950), as well as Blank (1954) and Fenichel (1946). In the opinion of these authors something in the realm of instinctual forces is defensively warded off. All the authors mentioned here, with the exception of Roth, who looked for a neurological explanation, used the psychoanalytic concepts at their disposal at the time. Meyer (1957, 1959) sees depersonalisation as a means of isolating a person from the outer world, a defensive phenomenon which, I suppose, could be seen as preventing the person from carrying out antisocial acts. Rudolf (1977) sees both depersonalisation and derealisation as having something to do with a schizoid disorder in development: depersonalisation and derealisation may be activated when a schizoid person has to deal with instinctual urges. Kernberg (1975) also thinks of such phenomena as being the result of developmental deficits in the ego. Renik (1972, 1978) regards depersonalisation and derealisation as primitive defence mechanisms. Like Bergler and Eidelberg (1935), Renik considers denial to be part of such a defensive manoeuvre, an idea in accordance with Freud (1927) who describes complex defensive manoeuvres with denial as a component.

My own understanding of depersonalisation and derealisation is close to that of Edith Jacobson (1949), with whom Kernberg (1975) also agrees. Depersonalisation can occur in healthy persons under extreme stress, and also in a person who is exposed to a hitherto unknown environment if this causes stress, which can induce regression. Regression can cause a conflict within the ego that prevents a person from dealing with the external situation in an adult way. In persons with a weak superego, this defence mechanism can also play a part in preventing instinctual forces from penetrating into the ego. One part of the ego tries to defend pre-existing ways of experiencing and behaving and another part of the ego, which is under the influence of regression and for this reason reacts in a more primitive way, reconstitutes former identifications which belong to the infantile past. One of the defence mechanisms employed by this part of the ego is primitive denial. According to Dorpat (1979), denial plays a central part in splitting, and in some cases can entirely explain the splitting phenomenon. I am close to this position.

Both depersonalisation and derealisation are changes in the ego that can occur when anxiety penetrates the defence barriers or arises in the ego. The anxiety is caused by an outside source, or it accompanies fantasies. In persons with a weak ego, anxiety breaks through and this can trigger depersonalisation or derealisation. Jacobson seems to think that no general ego weakness has to be present for a derealisation or depersonalisation to be triggered in extreme situations. With this position I concur on the basis of my own observations. Kernberg (1975) seems to have observed such phenomena only in persons with a general ego weakness. This may have something to do with the selection of patients. In the Menninger clinic, where Kernberg worked at that time, patients were probably more disturbed than those in the clinic where I worked.

Depersonalisation and derealisation are defence mechanisms which are employed when avoidance of a certain object or situation seems impossible, and are probably triggered when the defence mechanisms hitherto employed are no longer sufficient to allay severe anxiety. They prevent or reduce involvement with the outer world (Meyer, 1957, 1959).

The role of the superego

Many authors, for example, Deutsch (1928), Alexander (1930), Fenichel (1946), Wangh (1959), Ruddick (1961), Quint (1971), consider a deficiency in the phobic's superego to be co-responsible for a phobic patient's symptoms. An archaic superego can be warded off, as discussed by Kernberg (1975). If the defence does not work, a superego pathology may ensue, causing irrational self-blaming or the denial of real guilt. A well-developed superego, along with a directing object, can aid an overtaxed ego to keep antisocial impulses unconscious. It may also trigger defence mechanisms which had so far not been active, such as defences that lead to compromise formations typical of an obsessive-compulsive personality structure. One clinical concept developed before Kernberg (Dixon, de Monchaux, & Sandler, 1957) integrated adaptation to social realities and norms. This was, in a way, already contained in Hartmann's concept of adaptation to external reality (Hartmann, 1939).

A directing object directs a person to behave in a way that is socially competent, while the superego addresses the sector of morality, causing guilt feelings if its precepts are not followed. The ego ideal causes feeling of shame if a person does not conform to it. The directing object enables a person to act competently. If it does not function well, anxiety is experienced in social situations that demand actions that take the reality principle into account.

More on pre-oedipal causes of phobia

The authors mentioned above refer, in the main, to the oedipal phase of development as the time span when a disposition to becoming phobic is developed. Some also take a generalised ego weakness into account, without specifically addressing pre-oedipal phases of development. Other authors differentiate between pre-oedipal and oedipal aspects of phobic pathology. Post (1964), in a single case study, describes a patient with a mother who was always anxious. The patient felt close to his mother when he identified with her and felt anxious himself, but he also feared being "devoured" by her. On the other hand, he was afraid of losing her if he did not identify with her. Leaving his mother would have hurt her profoundly and losing his anxiety in analysis would mean losing the connection to his mother.

I have found similar dynamics in patients with cardiac neurosis but not in agoraphobia. Rhead (1969) describes agoraphobics who had not been able to develop beyond a child–mother symbiosis. He considers phobic behaviour as protecting patients from losing their connection to the mother, for this loss would expose them to situations where infantile sadomasochistic, exhibitionistic, or voyeuristic impulses might be triggered. This view is in some ways close to Bowlby's (1970). Khan (1966) and Rubinfine (1966), reporting on avoidant schizoid patients, describe patients whom Kernberg (1975) would have called borderline patients with phobic symptoms. Rycroft (1968) describes a difference between phobic and schizoid patients: schizoids move away from people, phobics move closer to them. However, this is only true for keeping closer to companions, not necessarily closer to people in general, who may be avoided. Hanna Segal (1954) describes a patient who presented schizoid and phobic symptoms. She supposes a combination of the two to occur in all agoraphobics; this is an overgeneralisation. Dallmeyer (1975) also describes combinations of schizoid and phobic symptoms, referring to various types of behaviour on the part of the mother that can lead to such combinations. A mother who rejects herself may also hate her children, extending self-hatred to hating what she has given birth to. Defensively warding off their own aggressive impulses, such mothers react by overprotecting the child.

The mother's relationship with the father is often precarious or downright bad. The father may show outbreaks of aggression and is then partly feared and partly despised. He often concentrates on himself and is not disposed to help the child or to provide stability for the family. This makes the mother cling to her small child, of whom she does not need to be afraid. Separation from each other is much feared by both mother and child, since the child has not learned to be independent of his mother and the mother may see the child as the only justification for her existence. Dallmeyer found a tendency to run away in patients who had experienced this kind of childhood. He explains this as a reaction to unbearable life situations, rooted in childhood and reproduced in adult life. Baumeyer (1959/1960) explains a tendency to run away as running away from both father and mother. Some of these patients are then tempted by a free-roaming, vagabond life with no stable relationship. On the other hand such a way of life is experienced as dangerous and anxiety-inducing. These patients wish for a harmonious way of relating to others, but want at the same time to be different from others and to not need anybody. (This can be seen as providing a narcissistic solution to problems experienced in relationships.) During the oedipal phase of development, such a child will have to choose between his parents, who are unable to provide a stable three-person relationship. But the child is unable to identify with one parent. He wants, rather, to leave, to run away. In psychotherapy, such a patient may experience an interpretation as an attack. In some cases, this may make the patient "run away" by terminating the therapy. Running away from a therapist then corresponds to a pre-formed way of behaving.

Frances and Dunn (1975) adopt concepts of object relations theory, with a conflict between autonomy and attachment: a child wants to remain close to its mother and losing this state of closeness generates anxiety. In this, they resemble Bowlby (1970), and also Rhead (1969). They also refer to Mahler (1971). In their description the child experiences a territory close to mother as safe, whereas being farther away is experienced as dangerous. The child wants his mother to remain connected to him, even at a distance, and to provide emotional refuelling. The child then returns to the mother from time to time, making contact and then leaving her to continue exploring.

Francis and Dunn (1975) see agoraphobic patients as behaving in a similar way. There is a territory where the patient feels safe. Agoraphobic symptoms serve to motivate a companion to stay with the phobic. Agoraphobic symptoms appear when triggered by a prospect of losing the companion or by changes in life situations that endanger the relationship. Aggressive impulses directed against the companion may be projected on to the environment, which is then experienced as even more dangerous. Francis and Duncan regard agoraphobia as a means of protecting a relationship. The relationship may be motivated in various ways, depending on the stage of development reached by the patient.

This ranges from a lack of self-object differentiation in psychotics to the relationship between two partners who are dependent on one another but are able to experience themselves as separate. Since the relationship then seems to be of value in itself, Francis and Dunn do not consider having a companion to be a substitute for having competencies. They regard inanimate objects that can serve as companions as having a symbolic meaning for the patient. For my part I consider such an inanimate object as preventing the patient from acting in a way that gets him into trouble.

Attachment

Bowlby (1973) considers separation anxiety as genetically determined: it can trigger reactions that enable a child to survive. He (Bowlby, 1970) sees the way agoraphobics look for a companion as a clinging to a mother substitute, caused by the patient's having experienced early separation from the mother or by having experienced an insecure relationship with the mother. Experiences of separation, in his view, cause aggression in the child. (I would add that aggression is also caused by a clinging or intrusive type A mother.)

Bowlby describes three types of family: one parent, usually the mother, is anxious and clinging, so clings to the child and prevents him from moving about. The child is afraid of losing his parents, for example when the parents fight; the child fears that something bad may happen if he goes away, so wants to stay at home; equally the parents fear that something bad will happen to the child, if he leaves the house (most frequently the case in school phobia, less so in agoraphobia).

Bowlby saw the development of self-confidence as depending on whether parents support the child, respecting the child's wishes, his capacity to act responsibly and his ability to acquire competencies in dealing with the outside world. For Bowlby, self-reliance did not mean autarchy; a self-reliant person asks for help when necessary and also helps others (Bowlby, 1970). Freud's (1926) idea that a child wants to be in the presence of his mother because he has *experienced* that his mother can banish the bad feelings caused by oral frustration, was not accepted by Bowlby, because he saw this behaviour as caused by genetics, not by experience. In phylogenesis, such behaviour has helped the child to survive.

I would agree with Hanly (1978); Bowlby's theoretical ideas are reductionist and too simple to help understand the complex set of factors which have an influence on the genesis of agoraphobia. I feel that his ideas should be supplemented with concepts drawn from object relations theory and ego psychology.

Whether attachment behaviour is learned or genetically determined is of great interest to psychoanalysts. Some think that if attachment were not learned but inherited, this would preclude psychodynamic hypotheses. Nevertheless, many kinds of behaviour do have a genetic component. For example, evolutionary psychology sees inborn programmes as co-determining partner choice (e.g., Buss, 1989), but this does not preclude partner choice being influenced by oedipal conflicts.

In psychoanalytic discussions we sometimes find a tendency to generalise without sufficient evidence. Bowlby himself did so when he practically excluded the influence of learning on attachment behaviour. On the other hand, excluding genetic factors can be the result of over-generalising the influence of learning.

The whole gamut of mental phenomena is produced by a combination of a person's inherited ways of experiencing the external world, of having an influence on it, and of being influenced by it. Certainly defence mechanisms are not learned; they are part of inherited ego functions. The same is true for the programmes postulated by evolutionary psychologists. Emotions, and their associated facial expressions, are not learned. But they can be blocked or exaggerated, and this varies from culture to culture. Ways of behaving can be learned by imitation or on the basis of identification. Thus, reacting with anxiety when confronted with the external world can be learned from the mother. This may or may not be beneficial, depending on whether the mother reacts in a realistic way. Anna Freud and Dorothy Burlingham (1971) observed that the intensity of children's anxiety during the bombings in World War II depended on how much anxiety their mothers showed.

Agoraphobia and free-floating anxiety

Free-floating anxiety not leading to phobic behaviour has been interpreted in various ways. Freud (1895) considers that the interruption of a cycle of sexual ecstasy could cause anxiety. Kernberg (1975) explains free-floating anxiety with a weakness in defence. Christian and Hahn (1964), Hahn (1975), and Fürstenau, Mahler, Morgenstern, Müller-Braunschweig, Richter, and Staewen (1964) consider the ingestion of toxic material and effects of infectious diseases as causing such anxiety.

However, free-floating anxiety may also mask agoraphobia when an unconscious impulse to run away is central. Leaving the house and so losing its protection would mean exposing oneself to dangerous situations. A house, however, cannot keep an agoraphobic person from running away in the way a human companion can. A patient may then report that he experiences anxiety "everywhere". Anxiety may, however, be more intense in the street than in the house. An unconscious wish for sexual intercourse with a known or unknown sex object may cause an agoraphobic to react with anxiety when doors (and sometimes windows) are not safely closed. A closed door may prevent persons from coming in, but it will not prevent the agoraphobic (who has a key) from leaving the house. Thus, asking the patient to describe the anxiety-triggering situations in detail may be helpful in finding out what it is the patient wants to do but is warding off defensively.

Hallen (1960) describes patients who produced intense anxiety after minor accidents. Hallen's view is that a narcissistic conviction of being absolutely safe is, as it were, destroyed by the experience that an unexpected accident can, in fact, happen. Such patients may have experienced great danger, for example, during a war, but in that situation they knew and took into account what might happen to them. Hallen regards these patients as having been symptom-free before the accident. The anxiety that is experienced when driving, after the driver has had an accident, and that seems more intense than could realistically be expected, may derive from aggressive impulses the patient is fending off. These may be directed at other drivers in a kind of counteraggressive reaction, their aggression being anticipated.

More about the agoraphobic's psychodynamics

Psychoanalysts usually concentrate on a phobic's conflicts or on the phobic's defensive manoeuvres, for example avoidance. Fenichel (1939) describes counterphobic symptoms as overcompensating for phobic anxiety. A counterphobic person does not avoid anxiety-generating situations. He looks out for them, for example, in sports. Thus, a phobic can either avoid, or can behave in a counterphobic way, which is the very opposite of avoidance.

Weissman (1966) sees a phobic's companion as a counterphobic object, in the sense that he counteracts anxiety. This is an idiosyncratic use of the term "counterphobic". In my opinion, the use of this term should be confined to a phobic's counterphobic behaviour.

Weissman reports a patient who had two companions, one at work and one in private life, always moving from one companion to the other. The anxiety he experienced on the way was bearable. When he considered separating from one of them, he experienced agoraphobic symptoms. Weissmann compares the companion to a fetish. A fetish enables a person to function sexually, a companion enables an agoraphobic to move about. He mentions a difference between a companion and a fetish: the fetish is a part object, the companion is a full object. But of course, in a way, the companion functions like a part object, being needed and used in a particular function. Terhune (1949) describes phobics with clear phobic symptoms, and most of these were agoraphobics. According to Terhune, the parents of these patients behaved in an anxious manner. Ternhune considers anxiousness to be, in a way, contagious. This is very close to what Anna Freud and Burlingham (1971) report and it tallies with my own observations.

Tucker (1956), who reports on outpatients from various social strata, found what he called a dependent personality structure in a large majority of patients. Unmarried women had a better prognosis in therapy, if a stabilised neurotic arrangement with a long-term partner did not exist. Nowadays, when many couples do not marry, this would include the long-term relationships of unmarried couples. In my own work, I have observed that the fear of losing a partner who functions as a companion may impede progress in therapy.

Dixon, de Monchaux, and Sandler (1957) differentiate between two types of danger: being impaired in social relations and having one's body impaired. The latter would cause castration anxiety, the former can cause the loss of objects. This accords well with my own observations, except for the fact that a fear of narcissistic impairment and a fear of guilt feelings may occur alongside a fear of object loss. The former occurs in phobics with a narcissistic streak, the latter in phobics with a depressive personality component.

Snaith (1968) compares agoraphobic patients to other phobics. According to what he observed, in agoraphobics avoidance occurs only when intense anxiety has been experienced, while other phobics avoided an anxiety-generating situation much earlier. In discussing this, it seems advisable to take the cost of avoidance into account. Avoiding an anxiety-provoking animal or avoiding great heights is easier than avoiding streets. Somebody who avoids great heights can probably do so without suffering much disadvantage. It is perhaps more difficult to avoid dogs. A claustrophobic who experiences anxiety when using a lift can use the stairs. However, not using streets confines you to your house or flat. So it seems probable that an agoraphobic will only stay at home if anxiety in the street becomes intolerable.

Snaith does not perceive agoraphobia as a real phobia. This is a matter of definition. In my definition, most phobic symptoms occur in a particular situation, such as being in a street or a public square, or in contact, often visual contact, with an object. This also applies to agoraphobia. Of course, avoidance can be generated by a traumatic experience. Somebody who has touched a hot stove will probably avoid doing it again. This is not a phobia according to my definition.

However, a combination is possible. An object that has caused a traumatic experience can be taken as a symbol. An internal object can be externalised on to an object that has already proved dangerous. Without this externalisation, the object would not have gained its anxiety-triggering properties. For example, a barking dog may appear to be dangerous and cause anxiety, but on closer acquaintance it may prove not to be dangerous. This dog just barks at strangers, without biting them. However, if the dog, because of the patient's bad past experience, invites the externalisation of internal dangerous objects, it may continue to generate anxiety.

Frazier and Carr (1967), in a textbook of psychiatry, come very close to describing what I think a companion is meant to do: to prevent a phobic person from transforming dangerous impulses into action. The companion is also expected to act like a devoted mother, preventing the accompanied person from doing things that could generate anxiety, which is how type A mothers of a phobic person often behave.

Frazier and Carr also refer to Helene Deutsch (1928), who sees the presence of a companion, acting as a mother substitute, as proving to the phobic person that he has not turned aggressive impulses, directed against mother, into destructive action.

The authors see anxiety in phobics as caused by their fear of being punished by a parent. This contrasts with my view: fear of punishment rather belongs to the obsessive-compulsive realm. In phobics, I see lack of social competence and fear of social ostracism as the central cause for anxiety. By contrast, these authors see fear of punishment as a factor preventing a child from becoming acquainted with justified fears, or experimenting with learning by trial and error, and thus learning to differentiate between fear that is justified by reality and dysfunctional fear. The authors also mention a fear of the body being destroyed, linking this to an infantile fear of being swallowed up. They mention that the child may then not become confident about his body, and will not understand impulses that are connected to the body. He will not learn to enjoy physical activities. This I would see rather as having something to do with the child being restricted in movement by a type A mother, but also by a type D mother, who does not support a child in learning by trial and error.

Willi (1972) addresses the marital relations of patients with anxiety symptoms. He describes his patients as unobtrusive and pleasant, but found it difficult to establish a working alliance, because the patients did not show the kind of verbal behaviour which could be addressed. They confined themselves to talking about their symptoms and wanted to satisfy the doctor, but expected him to tell them what to do.

The patients gave an impression of passivity, letting themselves be directed by outside forces; they did not try to structure the way they lived actively. Willi describes their mothers as anxious, preventing the formation of self-reliance, clinging to their children, fearing separation, trying to keep their children dependent on them. This, to a large extent, tallies with my views. As Richter and Beckmann (1969) report for patients with cardiac neurosis, some of their parents suffered from this syndrome. In agreement with these authors, Willi's view seems to be that the protective and nurturing functions of mothers were not integrated into the selves of his patients. They looked for substitute mothers, whom they expected to behave in an ideal way. According to Willi, people with anxiety symptoms chiefly want to preserve their symbiosis with the mother.

As children, Willi's patients were not able to develop sufficient ego strength to direct their own impulses and to integrate them. They feared being dominated by them if they admitted them into consciousness, and they avoided relationships that might trigger instinctual impulses. Willi saw their unconscious aggressive fantasies and impulses as still being in a primitive state of development, experienced as destructive, and destroying an adversary would mean destroying one's own life. In such patients, aggression is experienced as separating, it endangers symbiosis and cannot be experienced as permitting and enabling the development of solid relationships. The patient's amiable and obliging behaviour is explained by Willi as reaction formation. To my mind, this does not tell the whole story. In my experience, many phobic patients develop a genuine competence in adaptation that is superior to the average. They learn this by learning to "win" companions.

Richter and Beckman (1969), who address cardiac neurosis, consider an ideal mother object as integrated into the self representation. Willi accepts this view, but in my experience this is only true in cardiac neurosis. In agoraphobia, the mother object is deficient or insufficiently integrated, or both.

Also, Willi sees a general ego weakness, while, in my view, a general ego weakness only occurs in agoraphobics in whom a phobic personality structure is combined with borderline pathology. In such cases, a directing object may not be constituted because ego resources are not sufficient for this. Self-reliance is weak if a child does not do things in a way that satisfies a mother or mother substitute. A genuine lack of real competence combines with the introjection and, perhaps, integration of a devaluing mother object. Archaic aggression or archaic sexual impulses may result, if infantile aggression and infantile sexuality never reach consciousness, thus being excluded from a process of socialisation that occurs during childhood and adolescence. Of course, socialisation suffers when a very aggressive person, often a father, is part of the family. Dallmeyer (1975) makes similar observations.

Klemann, Kuda, and Massing (1975) observed that students at Göttingen University who had moved from a rural district into Göttingen often developed phobic symptoms. Indeed, most phobic students came from rural areas. Von Gebsattel (1959) reported that a village or small town may serve as what I would call a directing object (while a big town or a university town offers more freedom). Students from rural areas may not be equipped to deal with this. The village or small town had served as a directing object; Göttingen, a university town, offered less direction.

Prevalence

Patients' use of health services varies greatly. In a psychiatric hospital, there are fewer phobic patients than in a hospital that concentrates on psychotherapy and psychosomatics. In Germany, psychotherapists are concentrated in large cities and in university towns, less so in industrial regions such as the Ruhr valley. Most analysts or psychoanalytically oriented psychotherapists start their practice during training in a large city or university town and find it difficult to leave patients they are treating in long-term psychotherapy or psychoanalysis. They also want to stay in a place where discussion with colleagues is possible.

The number of psychotherapists in Germany has greatly increased since this book was first written, when many patients who could not find a psychotherapist in the place where they lived were treated in hospitals. Also, the state-supported insurance companies paid, and still pay, for inpatient treatment of people whose capacity to work seems in danger. Some patients think they should have hydrotherapy and perhaps do some sports and do not consider psychotherapy. Doctors who select patients to be admitted to a rehabilitation programme then propose a hospital where psychotherapy is offered. Thus, many phobic patients who would have been treated just with anxiolytic drugs by family doctors, now find their way to psychotherapy.

After a stay in hospital, they can continue therapy with a therapist in the place where they live. If they cannot find one, they may be readmitted to hospital after a period of two years. This is called interval inpatient therapy. The hospital where I worked while preparing and writing this book, had many such patients, who could have been treated in an outpatient setting. They came from all over West Germany.

Studt (1974) sifted through the epidemiological findings of various authors. The reported results vary greatly, which is not surprising, since the type of clients seeking treatment in a psychiatric or psychotherapeutic institution varies so much: it depends on the kind of services provided locally and on individual motivation and this, in turn, depends, among other things, on education and economic status.

In the hospital where I worked, the number of patients with phobias increased over the ten years during which I directed the department of clinical psychotherapy for adults, apparently for two reasons: I had started publishing on phobias, so we received more already diagnosed patients; and our own diagnostic work had improved. For example, we asked explicitly about phobic symptoms and found many patients with a phobic symptomatology who had not mentioned it spontaneously. Also, we discovered agoraphobias compensated for by a companion, and we looked for patients with a phobic personality component, but without clinically relevant symptoms.

Marks and Herst (1970) addressed 1500 members of a phobics' self-help organisation, ninety-five per cent of whom were female, using a questionnaire sent out to them, with a return of eighty per cent. In addition, they interviewed some members of the organisation and their relatives. Combinations of phobias with general anxiety, panic attacks, and depression were common. Combinations of agoraphobia with panic attacks were also common, as well as combinations with sexual disturbances and depression. Combinations of phobic symptoms with an obsessive-compulsive symptomatology were also found.

Marks and Gelder (1966) asked members of a phobics' association about the age of onset of their phobic symptoms: seventy-three women and eleven men with agoraphobia, eighteen patients with animal phobias, twelve patients with situational phobias (fear of heights, fear of darkness, fear of thunder), and twenty-five patients with social phobia were addressed. Animal phobias were reported to have started around age five; most situational phobias started in adulthood, but some before age five. Agoraphobia had a peak in late adolescence, and around age thirty. Most of the phobics had first consulted family doctors; sixty-seven per cent of them had also consulted psychiatrists. Members who had a sociophobic symptomatology found it difficult to ask anybody for help. Patients with animal phobias frequently consulted a doctor for other symptoms, such as depression, and mentioned their animal phobia more as an afterthought. All this tallies with my own observations.

I have frequently been asked whether the prevalence of anxiety syndromes has increased during the past three or four decades. This question is difficult to answer. Comparing studies several decades apart is fraught with methodological difficulties. The theoretical and methodological orientation of researchers and research methods change over time. Diagnostic criteria can vary greatly. The number of phobic syndromes diagnosed will depend on the number of psychotherapists available, on their training, and on progress in diagnostic work. It may increase or decrease as diagnoses become fashionable or fall out of fashion.

Have there been changes in the way people raise their children that might lead to an increase in the prevalence of phobic symptoms? Perhaps so. Life outside the home has become more dangerous for children because of increasing traffic. In towns and cities, children run increasing risks if they play in the street, so parents do have reasons to keep children inside the home, to warn them about the dangers of traffic, and not let them move about freely outside the home. On the other hand, even in earlier periods, children under three years of age were hardly ever left unsupervised. Mothers who work outside the home, and for whom no adequate substitute is provided, as is offered by good day-care institutions, may be forced by circumstances to behave like mothers of type D. Some mothers, whose children are cared for in day-care institutions, want to concentrate into the evening hours what a child may have missed during the day, overtaxing both the child and themselves.

The way children are brought up has changed during the past four or five decades. The desire of parents to practice a non-authoritarian style of parenting can make them draw back from their children, not wanting to appear authoritarian. Thus, the authoritarian behaviour of previous periods may be replaced by neglect. Such parents may also expect their children to behave in a rational manner when they are not yet able to do so. All this may result in type D mother behaviour.

There are more families with only one or two children. This seems to make the individual child appear more precious, and all the expectations parents may entertain will be concentrated on the one or two children they have. Parents may then overtax their children, expecting more developmental progress than a child can make. Here, again, there is a resemblance to type D behaviour.

Claustrophobia

Claustrophobia and agoraphobia can be present in the same patient. Claustrophobics are afraid of being in an enclosed space. Some places can trigger both claustrophobia and agoraphobia, for example, a department store, a cinema, a bus, a marketplace. These may be perceived as enclosed spaces but also as providing opportunities for meeting and interacting with people.

In claustrophobia, a patient experiences anxiety when enclosed in a confining space. Lewin (1935) illustrates this by referring to a short story by Edgar Allan Poe. Poe wrote about a man enclosed in a room whose walls moved inwards towards him, the room becoming more and more confining, and who was threatened by a knife swinging like a pendulum, descending on him. Lewin also describes the case of a woman patient who fantasised being a foetus in her mother's body. This fantasy did not cause anxiety. Anxiety was triggered when the patient developed a fantasy of a man, or a penis of a man, penetrating into the uterus from without. The patient then feared she would be hurt or driven out of the uterus. Lewin sees this in the context of theories of infantile sexuality. In a later paper, Lewin interprets a confined space as representing the insides of the mother's body, providing security. The walls of the confined space in the mother could, however, approach if the father lies on the mother, and it might be feared the father's penis would penetrate the uterus. Some patients also feared they might die of hunger in the confined space inside the mother. The choice of such a fantasy will depend on the way the mother was experienced in childhood. If she behaved in an oppressive way, the insides of her belly might be fantasised as oppressive. A mother's insides seen as being protective, without moving in an oppressive way, can cause fantasies of being secure.

Having experienced a bus or railway accident can lead a person to avoid buses or railway carriages. Hotels may be avoided if somebody has experienced a fire in a hotel. According to Salzman (1968), phobic anxiety states can, however, not be explained this way, since the intensity of anxiety generated in claustrophobia cannot be caused by such experiences alone. Snaith (1968) regards anxiety in phobics as being generated inside the patient, then being displaced on to an outside, plausible object or situation. Fenichel (1946) describes displacement in various phobic syndromes.

How can the concept of a directing object be applied to claustrophobia? And what kind of impulses could a directing object prevent from being transformed into action? At an early stage in life, when a child cannot yet differentiate a material object from a person, he hits or kicks a table he has inadvertently collided with, as if the table were an aggressive person. A child experiencing a mother who prevents him from moving about, may also experience a room in a house or flat where this takes place as belonging to his mother, connected with her or symbolising her. Most analysts will remember a regressed patient who experienced the consulting room as part of the analyst. A patient displacing his aggression from an internal object, frequently a mother object, can talk aggressively about the consulting room, before addressing the analyst herself. Displacement is not even necessary when the patient is regressed to a state when he experiences the analyst and her consulting room as being fused. In addressing the consulting room, he also addresses the analyst.

Similarly, a confined space or room may represent an oppressive or confining mother. This not only causes a feeling of being oppressed, it also causes aggressive feelings and impulses. Aggression is feared by the child, since it might destroy the mother or evoke counter-aggressive feelings in mother. This might mean losing her, and constitutes a danger of existential dimensions. The anxiety of the claustrophobic is thus caused by a fear of transforming aggressive impulses into aggressive acts. The aggressive impulses must be warded off. Anxiety reaches consciousness, but without the aggressive impulse itself. A similar situation is experienced by patients who suffer from cardiophobia. A cardiophobic patient fears for his own life. The mother object is unconsciously fantasised as fused with the patient's heart. In claustrophobics, mother is partly identified with a confined space or room.

Gehl (1964) examined patients in whom phobic symptoms alternated with depressive ones. When aggression was directed towards a confined space, it was not directed against the internal mother object. When anxiety became intolerable, it was reversed and directed towards the internal mother object, causing depression. When the anxiety that caused the unconscious aggressive feelings to be directed inwards diminished with time, aggression could be directed outwards again. Richter and Beckmann (1969) also report cases with a switch from symptoms of cardiac neurosis to symptoms of depression. Such mechanisms might explain this.

School phobia

Pittman, Langsley, and DeYoung (1968) compared avoidance in school phobia with psychological problems in the workplace in adults. They examined eleven patients, ten men and one woman. The woman lived in a homosexual relationship with a teacher whom she had avoided when she was a schoolgirl, so this was a special case.

All the men showed avoidance of work. As children, they had shown signs of a fully-fledged school phobia or had at least experienced anxiety when going to school. All the men were extremely dependent on their mothers or their wives, who encouraged them to stay at home. One wife left her husband when he started working but returned when he redeveloped anxiety concerning his work. Those showing signs of school phobia had stayed at home when their mothers felt anxious and lonely.

The authors described three solutions a person with school phobia may choose: a child who avoids going to school may stay with his mother right into adulthood and avoid work; a man can leave home, and marry a woman with whom he can have a relationship similar to a mother–child symbiosis; a wife can make her husband feel that he cannot cope with his work, which will make him avoid work. The authors regard school phobia as, in a way, resembling agoraphobia. Mothers or wives of school phobics seem to act similarly to the mothers and wives of agoraphobics.

Bowlby (1970) stresses separation anxiety rather than the anxiety-triggering situations a person may be exposed to outside the home. He mentions that symptoms of school phobia frequently diminish when the child arrives at school. This fits with the idea that teachers can be directing objects. Anxiety arises while the child moves from one directing object to another, from the mother to a teacher.

Skynner (1974) stresses the role of a father in helping a child to move out of the mother–child symbiosis. He may do this by his mere presence, but often some kind of activity on his part is necessary to foster the process of triangulation. If a mother–child symbiosis persists, this can result in school phobia.

Animal phobia

Animal phobia has little clinical relevance, since it is now possible, in most cases, to avoid the animal feared. Of course, a postman may lose his job if he does not enter buildings or gardens where there may be a dog, but this is an exception. Animal phobias have, however, caused much theoretical discussion.

One of Freud's (1909) case studies concerns a little boy, Hans, who developed a phobia of horses, an animal then often seen in the streets of Vienna. Some authors (such as Bräutigam, 1968) discuss inborn programmes, such as the fear of any kind of snake, which could be explained by the fact that some snakes are poisonous. Other authors discuss conditioning, for example, having been bitten by a dog and then fearing dogs, which in my definition has nothing to do with phobias, since a phobic person experiences disproportionate anxiety.

It is possible for animals to function as objects, on which an anxiety-generating internal object can be externalised. Some authors see an animal that generates anxiety as a symbol for a real person. Freud interpreted horses as being objects of displacement. In the case of Little Hans, they seemed to symbolise the father. Edith Sterba (1935) describes a case of dog phobia, the dog symbolising the phallic-aggressive father and the anal-invasive mother who gave enemas to the child. Helene Deutsch (1931) interprets cats as symbolising sadistic and masochistic impulses directed at women. Freud (1932) mentions spiders as symbols of a phallic woman. This was also mentioned by Abraham (1922) who, in addition, describes them as symbolizing a mother's phallus. Little (1967, 1968) considers spiders to have an oral symbolic meaning as well as the phallic one. Thus, spiders can symbolise a devouring mother. Spiders wait in hiding and then catch, envelop, and feed on the flies they have caught by sucking on them. According to Melitta Sperling (1971), when a patient mentions spiders, this points to a mother transference. Stiemerling (1973) reports that in some countries, spiders are thought to be evil human beings turned into animals by some kind of magic.

Renik (1972) does not consider an ability to symbolise to be necessary for the development of a phobia. When an object can be perceived as being separate and different from self, displacement can take place. For this, it is also necessary that a child can perceive similarity instead of thinking that one thing is just like another. Thus, a child in a Chinese restaurant may say that he wants to eat with pencils, meaning chopsticks (which are similar to pencils). The child the author mentions was fourteen months old. He mentions that a child of eighteen months might already be able to say that one thing *looks like* another. By contrast, Sarnoff (1970) considers the capacity to symbolise as a prerequisite for developing any kind of phobia.

I myself use the concept of a transference trigger (König, 1976), which I introduced when discussing transference in therapy groups. (A group may be experienced as a mother object, nourishing, confining, neglecting, obtrusive, etc.) Practically every transference is triggered by certain transference triggers. Greenson (1967) uses this term to denote an analyst's idiosyncrasies. I use it for all the pieces of information about an analyst that an analysand may have and that remind him of some person he knows or has known. These comprise the analyst's sex, age, looks, her way of reacting to the patient, the way of speaking, but also the house in which the analyst has the consulting room, the street where the house is situated, etc. The trigger may be very specific or quite general, such as the sex of the analyst. A phobic object also functions as a transference trigger.

How can we explain why the phobic object can cause more anxiety than is warranted by the real object? A phobic patient displaces unconscious aspects of an internal object which would cause much anxiety if perceived consciously. For example, conscious aggressive impulses directed against the father would have caused conscious anxiety in Little Hans, since the child probably also loved his father and did not only experience him as an adversary in the oedipal situation. Aggressive impulses directed against the mother often cause even more anxiety, she being experienced as a person without whom the child could not survive. Thus, the animal causing phobic anxiety need not to be a symbol according to Cassirer (1956), since the meaning of such an animal cannot be directly shared with other people. It has a special meaning for one person, the person who externalises a specific internal object or parts of it. The animal could be described as a sign, a sign being a property or a constellation of properties referring to something else. This is close to what Lorenzer (1970) seems to mean. However, Lorenzer thinks of a sign as being derived from a symbol by the repression of some of its properties. A transference trigger need not be derived from a symbol. An animal which triggers phobic anxiety resembles, by its properties or the properties ascribed to it, a specific object. Of course, symbolisation may play a part in this. But the patient does not need to be the author of such a symbol. He can simply take it from his language or culture.

The symbolic meaning of an animal has usually something to do with the animal's real properties, but these must not necessarily be the same as those that trigger the transference of different individuals. The specificity of transference triggers is derived from people's different biographies. Specific internal objects need specific transference triggers to touch off externalisation.

Animal phobias occur frequently in small children, and animal phobias in adults frequently persist from childhood. Why is this so? Fenichel (1946) talks of a child's animistic perception of an anxiety-generating animal. In it, human properties are ascribed to the animal. Animistic thinking is frequent in children. It gets weaker with time and rarely occurs in adults living in western societies. It probably can persist in the unconscious, as a part of primary process thinking.

In Arieti's view (Arieti, 1961/1962) the choice of such an object can depend on whether it is suitable to bind free-floating anxiety. Attaching anxiety to a concrete object makes the feeling easier to bear. The anxious person then seems to have found a reason for his anxiety. The animal seems to cause it. Whether this is the case can be decided by careful exploration of symptoms. Was there free-floating anxiety before the animal was considered to cause anxiety?

Acrophobia

In acrophobia, anxiety, often in combination with vertigo, is triggered in an elevated place, from which it is possible to fall. Acrophobic symptoms do not usually occur when the acrophobic person could not fall, as when looking through a window of an aircraft. In a cable car in the Alps, an acrophobic patient only felt anxiety when the conductor was not standing in front of the door, a position in which he would have been able to prevent the patient from opening it.

Why would anybody want to fall, or perhaps jump, from an elevated place, except if he wanted to commit suicide? The anxiety of the acrophobic is caused by a fantasy of being able to fly, as—possibly—in the young Winston Churchill, who jumped from an elevated place, thinking that he would land safely, which he didn't (Kohut, 1971). An unconscious fantasy, such as this, might have generated anxiety in a person who was not sure of being able to direct himself, not sure of being able to take reality into account. A person who is sure of this can enjoy such a fantasy if it becomes conscious. A patient with a narcissistic streak reported standing alongside the hull of a ship and looking at the water glittering in the sun. This somehow mesmerised her and she developed a fantasy of flying like a seagull, following the ship, and she enjoyed the fantasy. Had she been a phobic, the fantasy would probably not have become conscious, but would have triggered anxiety.

A patient with a phobic personality structure experienced his first anxiety attack when stepping on to a balcony on the sixth floor of the office building where he worked. This patient had a close relationship with a woman he did not marry, probably because of an ambivalent feeling towards her as a directing object. He experienced her as confining. A narcissistic component of his personality made him want to be entirely free, not dependent on anybody. When his mother died, with whom he also had a close relationship, anxiety did not appear. His partner was sufficient as a companion to him, but he now felt more dependent on her. This increased his ambivalence, causing unconscious aggressive feelings. He unconsciously wanted to leave his partner, but he could not do so because he needed her. In order to free himself from this conflict, he developed a fantasy of being reunited with his mother, and this led to a fantasy of jumping from the balcony into a garden, uniting with "mother earth". We know of such fantasies in suicidal patients. They can, indeed, lead to suicide by jumping from an elevated place (Henseler, 1975).

Jones (1913) reports a case of acrophobic symptomatology in a man that was only triggered when other men where present. Analysis showed that unconscious aggression against the father led to the unconscious fantasy of giving any man on to whom his father object was external-ised a push that would make him fall to his death. Baumeyer (1954) mentions an unconscious wish to return to the mother in the urge to let oneself fall. All kinds of conflicts have been discussed as causing acro-phobia (Fenichel, 1946; Ferenczi, 1922; Jones, 1912). An unconscious wish to be able to fly or to unite with the mother are, in my experience, frequent fantasies.

Goethe suffered from acrophobia. He seems to have experienced his first anxiety attack when mounting the steeple of Strasbourg cathedral, and he seems to have cured himself by training systematically to mount the steeple, a procedure behaviour therapists use even today. Acropho-bia does not often lead to therapy, since most people can easily avoid going to high up places. Acrophobics may remain anxiety-free in a high building if the windows are closed.

Cardiac neurosis

The symptoms of cardiac neurosis (Richter & Beckmann, 1969), or cardiopohobia (Kulenkampff & Bauer, 1960) or cardiac hypochondria (Bräutigam, 1968) are close to those of what Freud (1895) described as *Aktualneurose* or anxiety neurosis. He explained it by a disturbance of sexual satisfaction and never revised this, although during his lifetime Steckel (1924) had counted anxiety neurosis among cases of anxiety hys-teria and Jones (1912) considered that psychodynamic factors played a part in producing these kinds of symptoms.

Hahn (1975, 1976) makes a distinction between the anxiety attack, which can be produced by somatic factors and also by drugs like caffeine, and the resulting "phobic" avoidance concerning the place where the first anxiety attack had occurred. Blau (1952), who wants to keep the term *Aktualneurose*, explains this syndrome with a reduced capacity to tolerate anxiety-generating situations, due to some kind of ego weakness.

Fürstenau, Mahler, Morgenstern, Müller-Braunschweig, Richter, and Staewen (1964) examined thirty-five patients with cardiac neurosis, twenty-nine of whom were very dependent on their mothers. The patients felt they should not do anything which might endanger this relationship. Cardiac anxiety occurred when the patients wanted to do anything that could result in separation from the mother or at least might make the relationship less harmonious. When a partner threatened them with separation, they ascribed responsibility for this to themselves. The patients thought they would be unable to live without their mother or mother substitute, and they shared similar fantasies about their hearts. For them, a healthy heart was a good mother feeding their body with blood. The heart must not be endangered, for example, by lack of sleep or by toxic substances. Thus, the heart became a tyrannical object. The patients felt they had to do what this object wanted, and if they lost it they could not survive.

The authors name feelings and impulses that could endanger the relationship with the mother, for example, aggressive feelings directed towards her, or a wish to be like a father whom the mother hated. This was observed in patients with antisocial fathers. If the patients experienced a wish to become potent, self-reliant men, and not just a part of the mother, complementing her or serving as her ally in interpersonal conflicts, this resulted in anxiety. They did not feel permitted to engage in a sexual relationship, as that would have been unfaithful to the mother. Six patients were of a type that Richter and Beckmann (1969) named type B. They behaved in a phallic-narcissistic way, hiding their wishes for symbiosis with the mother.

So, the mother object in a patient with cardiac neurosis is fantasised as being located in the heart or fused with it. The patient feels directed by his heart. Were he not to follow its directions, he would run the danger of destroying it and killing himself. The mother object is an introject rather than an integrated part of ego structure. When this particular kind of directing object is projected, for example, on to a partner, everything the patient might do to anger or hurt the partner would, at the same time, endanger his heart. The directing object, which has remained in an infantile state, may be projected on to an adult patient's mother, thereby producing a relationship similar to that with his mother of childhood times. Cardiac neurosis can alternate with depression. When aggression towards the heart changes into aggression towards other, diffusely integrated parts of a mother-object, this results in depression.

Richter and Beckmann do not accept the term cardiophobia, because a person cannot avoid his own heart in the way an agoraphobic person might avoid the street. I myself find the term acceptable, since the patient avoids doing, and thinking, anything which might endanger his heart. A more precise, but probably cumbersome, description might express better the fact that what the patient avoids is any action that threatens his heart.

In agoraphobics, there is often a history of having been told they might hurt themselves by behaving in an expansive, adventurous, outgoing, rushing-around manner. By contrast, children who later develop a cardiac neurosis are often told that what they are doing might hurt their mother. Some mothers even tell the child that by misbehaving he might kill her.

Similarities, differences, and combinations

Phobia and obsessive-compulsive neurosis are in a way closely related (Benedetti, 1978; Freud, 1895a; Nagera, 1976; Quint, 1971; Salzman, 1968). Both ward off impulses that cannot be repressed. What is feared is loss of control. Avoidance is always part of a phobic pathology, but avoidance is not always a sign of phobia. (You may be bitten by a dog and try to avoid dogs for this reason.) In phobia, avoidance relates to unconscious wishes and fears. Salzman considers a feared object to be a symbol for something else, as, for example, a parental object. In my view, in a phobic person a feared object has something in common with an internal object. The patient projects or transfers a feared internal object on to the external object. Of course, symbols often do have something in common with what they symbolise. For example, a lion may symbolise aggression and/or power; a cock may symbolise pride. Salzman considers a symbolic meaning to be at the centre of phobic pathology. In my opinion, an internal object may be transferred to an external object that has a symbolic meaning from the start, such as a lion or a cock, but this is not necessarily so. The symbol may trigger the externalisation of an internal object because it shares some accidental properties with that object, but this would not trigger externalisation in a different person. For example, a person with a certain way of speaking, or speaking with a certain accent, can trigger the externalisation of an internal object relating to a person who speaks, or spoke, this way.

Also, the phobic object may be feared because it activates wishes, and these wishes may cause anxiety. A street may be experienced as a temptation to have sexual intercourse with strangers. In acrophobia, there is a temptation to jump and perhaps fly, and in this way make an unconscious narcissistic fantasy come true. At the same time, the acrophobic knows that he cannot fly like a bird and that he would perhaps kill himself if he tried to do so.

According to Salzman, stage fright can be caused by a fear of adverse reactions from people who are watching or listening. The fear is of a trauma causing a disturbance of narcissistic equilibrium. Some people are more sensitive to this than others. In my view, stage fright may also be caused by a lack of competence in dealing with exhibitionistic or aggressive tendencies and this generates a fear of losing control. Some people fear losing control more than others. In a play by the Austrian writer Peter Handke, the actors hurl insults at the auditorium. If this corresponded to what an actor—unconsciously—*really* wanted to do, the actor might experience anxiety, but would not insult the audience. In a theatrical performance, the actor reproduces a text and follows a director's instructions.

In Salzman's view, people with a narcissistic personality component will experience loss of control as a narcissistic injury. In this, they are similar to obsessive-compulsive people who also fear a loss of control. A phobic person, for Salzman, is fundamentally an obsessive-compulsive one. This is true in so far as both phobics and obsessive-compulsives fear loss of control, but they do so for different reasons. The obsessive-compulsive fears chaos; a phobic person fears behaving in a way that leads to social ostracism. Of course, combinations of the two may exist. In essence, phobic and obsessive-compulsive personality traits, developing at about the same time in childhood, are different ways of dealing with the danger of losing control.

In obsessive-compulsives, a need to control oneself, and also everything in the environment, is, according to Salzman, caused by a need to feel omnipotent. Self-control in obsessive-compulsives is, in his view, practised in various ways: taking a great deal of time to make decisions, desiring to do things just right, and also in isolation from affect and from the context. In all these the goal is to avoid mistakes. Thus, a fear of losing control, and the employment of procedures intended to gain and keep control, are common to both phobias and obsessive-compulsive neuroses but the ways a phobic person deals with this fear are different from those of an obsessive-compulsive person. A phobic person does not admit impulses into consciousness. He blocks them, only letting anxiety, which is a kind of hypertrophied signal anxiety, get through.

A phobic person can function normally if controlled by a companion. An obsessive-compulsive person would feel confined by relying on a companion of any sort, who would interfere with what he does, while a phobic person may unconsciously, and sometimes even consciously, feel confined but gain freedom of action when accompanied by a companion. Phobics have not learnt to deal with their own impulses in a competent way, so they are afraid to act if not accompanied by a companion. An obsessive-compulsive person feels forced to control himself and the environment, letting no other person play a determining role.

However, some obsessive-compulsives feel at ease in a hierarchy, obeying superiors if there is a compatibility of superego content. Of course, an obsessive-compulsive person will readily agree to assume control over persons lower down in the hierarchy.

Freud (1895b) observed that obsessive-compulsive and phobic symptoms can occur in the same person, without being able to explain the dynamics. Salzman attempts to explain them by considering phobics to be phobic-compulsive, because of the fear of loss of control that such a person shares with obsessive-compulsives. Salzman stresses what is common to the two, while I think it is more useful to look for specific differences, which can then be addressed in therapy. According to Salzman, the fear of losing control must be analysed, not the means of keeping control. In my view, both should be addressed. Salzman sees phobic symptoms as occurring when obsessive-compulsive defences are not sufficiently strong to keep control, in which case, avoidance becomes necessary. I have observed the contrary: obsessive-compulsive defences are employed when avoidance is no longer sufficient to allay anxiety. This occurs when the patient has no companion and when avoidance is not possible or not effective enough. Nacht (1966) observed the same sequence.

CHAPTER THREE

Further applications

Behavioural treatment of phobics—its psychodynamics

Even before the cognitive turn of behavioural therapy, this type of therapy did not confine itself to symptoms. Salzman (1968) supposes that behavioural therapy could lead to a displacement of symptoms, since the personality structure of a phobic patient remains unchanged. In fact, however, a personality structure may be changed by behavioural therapy and this can be explained by employing psychoanalytic concepts.

Behavioural therapists make their patients expose themselves to anxiety-triggering situations, in measured steps, in imagination or in reality. The therapist acts in a way that is different from the way the patient's mother did. As mentioned before, the mothers of phobic patients fall into two categories: type A mothers make the child avoid dangers; mothers of type D overtax the child by demanding competencies he was not helped to develop. (they show disappointment in a child who has not learned to deal adequately with impulses as competently as a child who has been helped to learn). In behavioural therapy, the patient experiences a mother figure (or mother substitute figure) who behaves in a different way from the original mother, thus providing a corrective emotional experience (Alexander & French, 1946; Alexander, reported in Zetzel, 1953). The development of an adequately functioning directing object is thus fostered by the therapist. It is for this reason that behavioural therapy leads to changes in personality structure. Additionally, the self-reliance of a patient is strengthened. He experiences less of the anxiety caused by a feeling of incompetence.

Alexander proposed a kind of role playing, with the therapist behaving in a way opposite to the patient's parent. This was not accepted by psychoanalysts, who demanded a more neutral kind of behaviour from the therapist. Neutral behaviour, accepting infantile fantasies and wishes, without, however, wanting to see them preserved, helps a patient to acquaint himself more with the reality principle. This, too, is different from the way a phobic's mother has behaved. This kind of corrective emotional experience is similar to what Kohut (1971) proposes for the treatment of narcissistic character neuroses. He does not refer to Alexander, whose ideas were difficult to accept on account of their manipulative component.

Nowadays, few analysts will refuse to admit that every kind of analyst behaviour can exert an influence, in analysis or in psychotherapy. Kohut sees the experience that an analyst provides as deriving from empathy. But, of course, by showing empathy, an analyst will be behaving in a way different from an unempathic parent, thereby providing a corrective emotional experience without role playing.

In Kohut's view, a corrective experience consists in the patient's experiencing a therapist who strives for empathy (but does not always succeed). In behavioural treatment, a corrective emotional experience is provided by the therapist behaving in a way different from the way a phobogenic mother behaved, providing an alternative that helps, with time, to constitute a better directing object. I consider this idea to be important since, as I mentioned before, this explains the undoubted effects of behavioural therapy in terms of psychoanalytic concepts.

The relationship of phobic persons to a directing object is always ambivalent. The aggressive element in the ambivalence can prevent the directing object from being integrated into the self. Then, it can easily be externalised, as I have described in the section on cardiac neurosis. According to Kohut (1971), patients with a narcissistic personality structure may transfer ideal parental imagoes to the analyst. An ideal object can also become part of the self by identification.

In narcissistic persons, we find problems in the evaluation of self. In phobic persons, competence in dealing with the drives is under-developed. If an ideal self-object is externalised by a narcissistic person, this has beneficial effects on self-evaluation. In phobics, the externali-sation of the directing object can increase competencies in dealing with impulses originating in the drives. When, in therapy, the internal directing object becomes more competent, this has consequences for the patient's self-evaluation.

Substitute objects in other fields of psychopathology

In depressives, an external emotional nurturing object may be wanted. A well-integrated internal mother object can help a person to nurture himself emotionally. A mother object that was only introjected cannot do this. A depressive person might look for somebody to supply emo-tional nurture from the outside.

The substitution can also be for body parts. A man may substitute for a woman's phallus. Her unconscious idea that she lacks a penis is derived from identification with a man in the family of origin, often based on a relationship with the father experienced as more emotion-ally satisfying than the relationship with mother. Identification with the father may also be preferred because the position of the father in the family was more attractive than the position of the mother. The woman experiences herself as lacking a penis since it is supposed to denote, or symbolise, attractive maleness.

Men who remain identified with the mother are unsure about the qualities of their penis. Some of these develop what is called a phallic-narcissistic personality structure, looking for objects that admire their maleness. In the Appendix, I describe other ways of developing a personality structure of this kind. A phallic-narcissistic woman identified with the father may motivate her partner to prove his maleness by succeeding in male endeavours. Of course, she could also want to prove that she is as good as, or better than, successful men. I assume that in Freud's time, more women wanted a man as a substitute phallus than they do now, because women of that period had little opportunity to compete directly with men. Outstanding personalities and women born into a leading role, such as female monarchs, were the exceptions.

In a woman, there is no real defect that could be compensated for by substitution. It is a fantasised defect due to an identification with a person of the opposite sex.

Masochism

Masochism can occur in combination with a phobic character structure. In therapy, a masochist patient may experience a therapist's interventions as sadistic penetrations. Masochistic patients try to provoke the analyst, wanting him to act in a way they can experience as sadistic. A child developing a masochistic character structure may, by the transgression of norms, provoke punishment by his parent. Thus, not complying with norms becomes part of a masochistic arrangement. The masochistic child may want to be punished because he takes the punishment as proof that the punishing parent cares for him; later on, this will perhaps be experienced on an adult sexual level. The masochistic child, having integrated a blaming and punishing parent, will show a tendency to blame himself and, self-blaming is enjoyed.

In a masochistic perversion, interpersonal relationships may be confined to sadomasochistic interactions. Masochists may provoke a partner in order to be punished. They will, however, avoid endangering the relationship; this is a matter of dosage. It is hoped the partner will make clear what will only lead to punishment and what will make him or her leave or act destructively, overstepping the limits of the sadomasochistic arrangement. Thus, in a way, the masochistic partner is used as a directing object. The sadistic partner may also want to control what the masochistic person does, or does not, do outside the relationship. Then he can function as a directing object in a more general way.

A twenty-three-year-old woman entered inpatient therapy because she rocked herself, like an autistic child. During an admission conference she readily demonstrated this squatting down and rocking, which then caused members of the team to ask her about her sex life. In demonstrating the rocking, she gave the impression of being bound hand and foot. When she had left the room, there was a discussion about the diagnosis—was the symptom simply an autistic one or was there some sexual content? It later became clear that as a child the patient had rocked herself in bed. Her father, who wanted her to stop doing this, used to hit her. Later, she recounted sadomasochistic behaviour that she practiced with her partner by mutual consent. In the course of therapy this relationship was labilised. The patient then experienced considerable anxiety. If there is a manifest and consensual sadomasochistic relationship the masochistic partner does not really have to provoke the sadistic partner to treat him or her sadistically. Since the relationship with the sadistic partner remained stable after all, the patient felt no need to provoke people in the hospital. Once, however, she left without permission, in order to visit her partner. She had experienced a great deal of anxiety and wanted to make sure that the relationship with her partner still existed. Masochistic perversions are frequently rationalised as serving the "education" of the masochistic partner. The young woman, in her professional life, was in an educator's role, perhaps in identification with the sadistic father.

More on free-floating anxiety, developmental pathology, qualities of the relationship with a companion, and social phobia

Phobic anxiety and free-floating anxiety are produced in different ways. Phobic anxiety has something to do with an insufficiently developed internal directing object. In free-floating anxiety the ego is underdeveloped in a more general way, but which can and usually does also concern the internal directing object. Studt (1984) demonstrated, in an empirical study, that patients with free-floating anxiety show more developmental pathology then patients with phobic anxiety. Rohde-Dachser (1983) and Kernberg (1975) found pre-psychotic structural components in patients with free-floating anxiety.

Patients with developmental pathology can find it difficult to sustain reliable relationships with persons who are reliable. They may also find it difficult to judge the competencies of a prospective external directing object. An external object serving as a directing object is primarily needed for its directing functions. The relationship to such an object is, however, usually more stable if the relationship does not confine itself to these functions. A person who has reached the depressive position according to Melanie Klein's definition, and is thus able to tolerate good and bad in one person, will usually develop more stable relationships than somebody who has not reached the depressive position. Frequently phobic patients with type D mothers have not reached this stage of development. For such persons, inanimate objects, serving as directing objects, may prove more reliable than humans.

Erythrophobia is frequent in patients with developmental pathology. I have often observed it in patients who come from families where a parent behaved in a way which was considered something to be ashamed of, such as drinking too heavily or committing criminal actions. One patient was ashamed of his father, who was a clergyman, because he had found books with pornographic content in his father's library, bound in black covers like his theological books. The patients are partly identified with such parents. Also, a child may be ashamed of parental behaviour that is considered to be acceptable in a certain social class, but not in another where the child spends a lot of time, for example, upper class behaviour in a school where most, or all, of the children come from lower class families.

Counselling

There are a phobic people who cannot work at all without a companion, but with a companion they can. This could be treated by classical psychoanalysis or some shorter variety, such as dynamic psychotherapy, but both take a certain time, which is not always available. With university students, I have had some success using counselling. For example, I asked a phobic student to do his work in the university library, where there were students he could ask when in difficulty. He was then able to work, without asking anybody, like the university professor I have mentioned elsewhere who could not write his papers without having his wife present.

A middle-echelon manager was promoted to a higher level in the hierarchy, where it was necessary to make far-reaching decisions, which caused him disproportionate anxiety. I asked him to talk with his staff when any decision was pending which he found difficult. These members of staff were not more competent then he was, but they formed a group of companions. To motivate him, I reminded him of the fact that cabinet ministers and prime ministers usually have staff to advise them. This helped the manager to accept counselling from his staff members. And, incidentally, he was praised for his democratic leadership style.

APPENDIX

Personality structures

The reader may wish to be informed about personality structures in general. The following is based on Riemann's (1961) work which I developed further (König, 1992, 2004) and have used in books on technique (e.g., 1995a, 2001, 2007) and in a book on psychological and mental health problems in the workplace (2011).

In schizoid persons, the main conflict is between a wish to fuse with an object and a fear of losing one's identity by doing so. There is developmental arrest at a symbiotic stage of development. An ego development which enables a person to look at an object and perceive in detail what it is like has not yet, or has only partly, taken place. Schizoid people want to be close to people and want also to keep at a distance from them. External reality does not interest them much; they turn to introspection. They have no full relationship with any object. Schizoid persons relate to what they project on to people; you might say they interact with parts of their own projected self. Schizoids are inclined to experience love at first sight, falling in love with fantasised parts of their own self if they find a person who appears to be similar to them in some important way.

A schizoid character structure predisposes a person to abstract thinking. Any kind of work which calls for attention to detail is experienced as difficult, or is impossible to do. In character, in this respect, they are the opposite of people with an obsessive-compulsive personality structure, who pay a great deal of attention to detail but find it difficult to perceive connections between them.

Narcissistic people overestimate their own importance and underestimate the importance and value of others. As in schizoids, there is no whole-object relationship. A person is perceived as a constellation of functions the narcissistic person needs or does not need. One of the object's functions that is important to narcissistic persons is the other person's admiration of them. This stabilises their high self-evaluation, which is always in danger of being proven wrong by confrontations with reality. Narcissistic people cannot keep admiration provided by others in storage: it is as if they had developed no receptacle for it, or only a very small one; they lacked admiration by others in their childhood. For this reason, admiration has to be as continuous as possible. In old age, some of them surround themselves, as many actors do, with memorabilia of former success, as a substitute for admiration. Any object which does not fulfil the desired functions is dropped. A narcissistic person, stabilised by admiration, can do good and even excellent work, but he cannot have full relationships of any kind with people.

Persons with a *depressive* personality structure are, in some ways, the opposite of those with a narcissistic character structure. They underestimate themselves and overestimate others. People with a depressive character structure feel dependent on objects who feed them in some way. Many feel that they cannot survive by themselves. This leads to a great dependence on external objects. Since people are very important to them, depressively structured individuals are over-represented in the helping professions. Dependence motivates them to study the objects and attend to their needs, often by feeding them, literally or in a metaphorical sense. They have difficulty starting work, since they lack initiative, which was blocked early in life. The first initiative of a baby consists in searching for the breast. A mother may facilitate this, or make it difficult and frustrating. To stop working is also difficult, because they are afraid of not being able to start again. They are rather like a car without a battery to provide electric current. So they need to be pushed in order to start the motor, and if they stop they need to be pushed again.

The relationships of depressively structured people are concentrated on meeting the wishes of the partner while neglecting their own interests and needs. Since the extent to which depressively structured persons desire to be cared for in their turn is great, they will frequently experience deficits. This situation will arouse aggression, which they will turn against themselves in order to keep the object safe. This may result in depression. Likewise, the loss of an object may trigger depression. However, being depressed is not a necessary component of the depressive structure; the structure merely disposes a person to depression.

People with an *obsessive-compulsive* personality structure suffer from conflicts between a desire for safety and the wish to put impulses that could cause a chaotic situation into practice. They ward off this wish, and this defence restricts the range of their possible actions and reactions. Such people appear to be caught in a rigid framework, often determined by the contents of the superego. They pay great attention to detail, but they cannot see how the details are related. This is prevented by a defence mechanism known as "isolation from context". Obsessive-compulsives as scientists collect great quantities of data, which they could put to use if they were able to see how they are related. Since they cannot do this, they produce what is called a "data cemetery". If the ego, often helped by a rigid superego and employing defence mechanisms, cannot prevent such chaos-creating impulses from entering consciousness, the contents that come through are often devoid of any affect that might motivate the person to put the impulse into action. This is due to the defence mechanism "isolation of/from affect". Isolation from context can allow the impulses to come through without the context that motivates them. They appear absurd to the person who experiences them.

Checking on one's actions by repeating them over and over again can prevent a person from working productively, working time being spent in checking. People of this kind are not sure of themselves. They feel their checking-up may be faulty, so they repeat it. Most people who are not obsessive-compulsive check once, or perhaps twice, and are then satisfied. Since change may always result in things that obsessive-compulsives cannot have foreseen, they will resist change, often change of any kind.

The obsessive-compulsive personality structure is a good example of personality having positive as well as negative aspects. For example,

Germans are said to produce reliable cars. In the production of cars, spontaneity and new ideas that might change the process may, if put into immediate action, result in chaos, or at least in a lack of reliability in the product. In Germany, as in Japan, ideas for change are channelled in a way that is designed to make them become useful. There are people whose job is to receive and check proposals for change and to select the potentially useful ones; these are appropriate positions for those with an obsessive-compulsive personality structure.

The *phobic character structure* has been extensively described in this book, and combinations with an obsessive-compulsive character structure have also been addressed.

A *phallic-narcissistic* personality structure makes a person unsure of his gender. Around the fourth year of life, when a child's interest starts to focus on sex differences, he will establish hypothetical links between being of a certain sex and being accepted as a person. A boy who does not feel accepted may feel that he is not accepted as a boy, perhaps because he does not display manly enough behaviour, perhaps because he is still too much identified with his mother. He may also feel less manly than his father and is not prepared to take up oedipal rivalry. On the other hand, parents may concentrate on the main characteristics of a boy, encouraging him to behave in a manly way and mentioning his male characteristics on every occasion. This may make the boy feel that he is only accepted because he is male, thus gaining the impression that other aspects of his personality are not important in comparison to his being male. He will then cultivate his maleness and feel that being loved depends exclusively on this.

A girl may be praised for feminine characteristics, or feminine characteristics may seem to be considered unimportant, but when she behaves more like a boy this may be better received. For example, the parents may have wanted the child to be a boy rather than a girl. A father who wanted a boy may praise the girl when she behaves like one, while the mother in this family may have wanted a girl and praises the child when she behaves in a feminine way. This may cause a girl to be unsure about her gender.

Other factors may also come into play. For example, the father's position in the family can seem more attractive than the mother's. This contributes to making the girl want to be a boy. In a family where the positions are reversed, the mother's position seeming more attractive, a boy may want to be like his mother.

Hormonal conditions, such as the amount of testosterone in the child's body, may, of course, also have an influence on gender identification. In adult life, men unsure of their gender will cultivate their manliness. This may result in a kind of "macho" behaviour. Such men will always be on the lookout for people who admire them for their manliness. A man more than usually identified with his mother may, in western society today, feel even more obliged to behave like a man, because men who behave rather like women are not universally accepted. They are accepted in some sections of society but this attitude is mostly confined to artists and intellectuals. In our society as a whole, younger people are more accepting of a man who shows some kind of feminine behaviour than are older ones.

Women who behave rather like men are much more accepted. As a result, many women feel free to live the way they feel as to gender characteristics. They behave more like men if they are identified with a male type of person. Women identified with the classic feminine role will want to live accordingly, which may cause interpersonal conflicts in a society where classic feminine behaviour is perhaps on the way out. This seems to be true among young middle-class people. Also, women who have been particularly appreciated for their femininity may tend to put all their eggs into the one basket of erotic attraction, which does not entirely conform to what most men nowadays expect of women.

A *hysterical (histrionic)* personality structure of the oedipal type develops during the oedipal phase, which follows upon the phallic-narcissistic stage (the phallic-narcissistic structure could also be termed hysterical, since it derives from conflicts concerning sex differences and gender). In men and women who have stayed stuck in the oedipal phase, oedipal conflicts continue to be at the forefront of their minds. This prevents them from using a time window that opens in cognitive development during the fifth or sixth year of life, which is the period when cognitive development takes place in rational thinking, planning, and in the postponing of actions, if rational thinking prior to action is needed or useful. All this is only partially developed in a person with a hysterical personality structure. Like a child of the oedipal phase, such a person likes to move on to something new and soon gets bored with routine.

Oedipal conflicts that can lead to arrested development are well known. In a form termed positive, a boy wishes to take his father's place at his mother's side and fears his father's counter-aggression. In a variation termed negative, the sexes are reversed: the boy wishes to take the mother's place and fears her counter-aggression. In girls, the sexes are reversed.

It is important to take into account, when considering all this, that the child does not really want to lose or even "kill" his father; children at this age want to keep the parental couple intact. He just wants to change places, without making the father disappear altogether. Ideally, from the child's point of view, the parent whose place a child wants to take should concede it; the parent in question should accept the child as stronger, or more attractive, or both.

However, if parents behave in a way that makes the child think he has attained his goal, this has untoward effects in later life. As an adult, he will feel that being accepted as a more attractive partner is the most important thing in life rather than being motivated to develop adult competencies, since in the child's eyes these qualities seem to have been of no use to the parent he has supplanted during the oedipal struggle.

In earlier periods of history, for instance in Jane Austen's time, a woman's ideal career consisted in being married to a man of (preferably) high status, while most men were expected to be competent in their field of work or station in life and to acquire, or maintain, material status and resources. Though much has changed since Jane Austen's day, it is interesting that transcultural research (Buss, 1989) seems to have shown that physical attractiveness and status still, to a large extent, dominate in partner choice, even in western industrialised societies.

ICD-10

In the ICD-10 (WHO, 1992), various types of personality and behaviour disorder are classified. Some of them can be seen as extreme forms of character structures. The schizoid personality disorder, the histrionic personality disorder, and the anankastic personality disorder are extreme forms of schizoid, hysterical, and obsessive-compulsive character structures. The anxious or avoidant personality disorder and the dependent personality disorder do not directly correspond to psychoanalytic character types. However, the depressive character type corresponds in some ways to the dependent personality disorder.

A phobic personality disorder is not listed in the ICD-10; people with a phobic personality structure are usually categorised in the anxious and the dependent personality category. The better heading can well be applied since a phobic person is *dependent* on a companion.

The term dependent personality disorder fits better with what in psychoanalysis is often called depressive personality without depression. It predisposes to depression, but there are many people with such a personality structure who have never become depressed, because they were never exposed to specific triggering situations, such as the loss of an object. The dependence upon a companion is of a different kind. The loss of a companion usually generates anxiety, not depression.

A narcissistic character structure is mentioned in the IDC-10, under the rubric F60.8.

REFERENCES

Abraham, K. (1913). Zur Psychogenese der Straßenangst im Kindesalter. In: *Karl Abraham—Psychoanalytische Studien, Vol. 1* (pp. 41–42). Frankfurt/ Main: Fischer, 1971.

Abraham, K. (1914). Über eine konstitutionelle Grundlage der lokomotorischen Angst. *Internationale Zeitschrift für Psychoanalyse, 2*: 143–150.

Abraham, K. (1921). Äußerungsformen des weiblichen Kastrationskomplexes. *Internationale Zeitschrift für Psychoanalyse, 7*: 422–452.

Abraham, K. (1922). Die Spinne als Traumsymbol. *Internationale Zeitschrift für Psychoanalyse, 8*: 470–475.

Alexander, F. (1930). *The Psychoanalysis of the Total Personality.* New York: Nervous and Mental Disease Publishing Company.

Alexander, F., & French, T. (1946). *Psychoanalytic Therapy.* New York: Ronald Press.

Arieti, S. (1961/62). A re-examination of the phobic symptom and of symbolism in psychopathology. *American Journal of Psychiatry, 118*: 106–110.

Arlow, J. A. (1979). Metaphor and the psychoanalytic situation. *Psychoanalytic Quarterly, 48*: 363–385.

Balint, M. (1956). Pleasure, object and libido. Some reflections on Fairbairn's modifications of psychoanalytic theory. *British Journal of Medical Psychology, 29*: 162–167.

Baumeyer, F. (1950). Zur Kasuistik und Theorie der Straßenangst. *Psyche: Zeitschrift für Psychoanalyse, 1*: 164–179.

Baumeyer, F. (1954). Der Höhenschwindel. *Nervenarzt, 25*: 467–473.

Baumeyer, F. (1959/1960). Zur Symptomatologie und Genese der Agoraphobie. *Zeitschrift für Psychosomatische Medizin und Psychotherapie, 6*: 231–245.

Benedetti, G. (1978). *Psychodynamik der Zwangsneurose*. Darmstadt: Wissenschaftliche Buchgesellschaft.

Bergler, E. (1951). The Marshal Ney formula. *The Psychoanalytic Review, 38*: 172–179.

Bergler, E., & Eidelberg, L. (1935). Der Mechanismus der Depersonalisation. *Internationale Zeitschrift für Psychoanalyse, 21*: 258–285.

Blank, H. R. (1954). Depression, hypomania and depersonalization. *Psychoanalytic Quarterly, 23*: 20–37.

Blau, A. (1952). In support of Freud's syndrome of "actual" anxiety neurosis. *Internationale Zeitschrift für Psychoanalyse, 33*: 363–372.

Bowlby, J. (1970). *Attachment and Loss, Vol. I, Attachment*. London: Hogarth.

Bowlby, J. (1973). *Attachment and Loss, Vol. II, Separation: Anxiety and Anger*. London: Hogarth.

Bräutigam, W. (1968). *Reaktionen, Neurosen, Psychopathien*. Stuttgart: Thieme.

Buss, D. (1989). Sex differences in human mate preferences. Evolutionary hypothesis tested in 37 cultures. *Behavioral and Brain Sciences, 12*: 1–49.

Cassirer, E. (1956). *Wesen und Wirkung des Symbolbegriffs*. Darmstadt: Wissenschaftliche Buchgesellschaft, 1969.

Christian, P., & Hahn, P. (1964). Psychosomatische Syndrome im Gefolge internistischer Erkrankungen. *Der Internist, 5*: 163–171.

Dallmeyer, H. J. (1975). Zur Psychodynamik des Weglaufens angstneurotischer Patienten. (unpublished).

Deutsch, H. (1928). Zur Genese der Platzangst. *Internationale Zeitschrift für Psychoanalyse, 14*: 297–314.

Deutsch, H. (1931). Ein Fall von Katzenphobie. In: A. J. Storfer (Ed.), *Almanach der Psychoanalyse* (pp. 135–147). Wien: Internationaler Psychoanalytischer Verlag.

Dixon, J. J., de Monchaux, C., & Sandler, J. (1957). Patterns of anxiety: the phobias. *British Journal of Medical Psychology, 30*: 34–40.

Dorpat, T. L. (1979). Is splitting a defense? *International Review of Psycho-Analysis, 6*: 105–113.

Fairbairn, W. R. D. (1952). *An Object-Relations Theory of the Personality*. New York: Basic Books.

Federn, P. (1956). *Ichpsychologie und die Psychosen*. Frankfurt/Main: Suhrkamp, 1978.

Fenichel, O. (1939). The counter-phobic attitude. *International Journal of Psycho-Analysis, 20*: 263–274.

Fenichel, O. (1944). Remarks on the common phobias. *Psychoanalytic Quarterly, 13*: 313–326.

Fenichel, O. (1946). *The Psychoanalytic Theory of the Neurosis*. London: Routledge & Kegan Paul.

Ferenczi, S. (1922). Die Brückensymbolik und die Don Juan-Legende. In: *Bausteine zur Psychoanalyse, Bd. II* (pp. 244–246). Bern: Huber, 1964.

Ficarra, B. J., & Nelson, R. A. (1946/47). Phobia as a symptom in hyperthyroidism. *American Journal of Psychiatry, 103*: 831–832.

Fonagy, P., Cooper, M., & Wallerstein, R. S. (1999). *Psychoanalysis on the Move: The Work of Joseph Sandler*. London: Karnac.

Frances, A., & Dunn, P. (1975). The attachment-autonomy conflict in agoraphobia. *International Journal of Psycho-Analysis, 56*: 435–439.

Frazier, S. H., & Carr, A. C. (1967). Phobic reaction. In: A. M. Freedman & H. I. Kaplan (Eds.), *Comprehensive Textbook of Psychiatry* (pp. 899–911). Baltimore: Williams & Wilkins.

Freud, A. (1936). *The Ego and the Mechanisms of Defence*. London: Karnac, 1993.

Freud, A. (1977). Fears, anxieties, and phobic phenomena. *Psychoanalytical Study of the Child, 32*: 85–90.

Freud, A., & Burlingham, D. (1971). *Heimatlose Kinder. Zur Anwendung psychoanalytischen Wissens auf die Kindererziehung*. Frankfurt/Main: Fischer.

Freud, S. (1895a). Obsessions: Obsessions and phobias. Their physical mechanism and aetiology. *S. E., 3*: 71–83. London: Hogarth.

Freud, S. (1895b). On the grounds for detaching a particular syndrome from neurasthenia under the description "anxiety neurosis". *S. E., 3*: 87–117. London: Hogarth.

Freud, S. (1908). Character and anal eroticism. *S. E., 9*: 167–180.

Freud, S. (1909). Analysis of a phobia in a five-year-old boy. *S. E., 10*: 3–149. London: Hogarth.

Freud, S. (1917). Mourning and melancholia. *S. E., 14*: 237–258. London: Hogarth.

Freud, S. (1926). Inhibitions, symptoms and anxiety. *S. E., 20*: 75–172. London: Hogarth.

Freud, S. (1927). Fetishism. *S. E., 21*: 147–158. London: Hogarth.

Freud, S. (1932). Revision of the theory of dreams. *S. E., 22*: 7–30. London: Hogarth.

Fürstenau, P., Mahler, E., Morgenstern, H., Müller-Braunschweig, H., Richter, H. -E., & Staewen, R. (1964). Untersuchungen über Herzneurose. *Psyche, 18*: 177–190.

Gebsattel, V. E. von (1959). Die phobische Fehlhaltung. In: V. E. Frankl, V. E. von Gebsattel & J. H. Schultz (Eds.), *Handbuch der Neurosenlehre und Psychotherapie, Bd. II* (pp. 102–124). München: Urban & Schwarzenberg.

Gehl, R. H. (1964). Depression and claustrophobia. *International Journal of Psycho-Analysis*, 45: 312–323.

Greenson, R. R. (1967). *The Technique and Practice of Psychoanalysis*, Vol. I. New York: International Universities Press.

Guntrip, H. (1961). *Personality Structure and Human Interaction: The Developing Synthesis of Psychodynamic Theory*. London: Hogarth.

Guntrip, H. (1968). *Schizoid Phenomena, Object Relations and the Self*. London: Hogarth.

Hahn, P. (1975). Sympathicovasaler Anfall und Herzphobie. *Materialien zur Psychoanalyse und analytisch-orientierten Psychotherapie* II (3), Sektion C, Heft 11. Göttingen: Vandenhoeck & Ruprecht.

Hahn, P. (1976). Die Bedeutung des „somatischen Entgegenkommens" für die Symptombildung bei der phobischen Herzneurose. *Therapiewoche*, 26: 963–966.

Hallen, O. (1960). Über isolierte Phobien nach Verkehrsunfällen. *Nervenarzt*, 31: 454–462.

Hanly, C. (1978). A critical consideration of Bowlby's ethological theory of anxiety. *Psychoanalytic Quarterly*, 47: 364–380.

Hartmann, H. (1939). *Ich-Psychologie und Anpassungsproblem*. Stuttgart: Klett, 1970.

Henseler, H. (1975). Die Suizidhandlung unter dem Aspekt der psychoanalytischen Narzißmustheorie. *Psyche*, 29: 191–207.

Hoffmann, S. O. (1979). *Charakter und Neurose*. Frankfurt/Main: Suhrkamp.

Jacobson, E. (1949). Observations on the psychological effect of imprisonment on female political prisoners. In: K. R. Eissler (Ed.), *Searchlights on Delinquency* (pp. 341–368). New York: International Universities Press.

Jones, E. (1912). The relation between the anxiety neurosis and anxiety hysteria. In: *Papers on Psychoanalysis* (pp. 513–520). London: Balliere, Tindall & Cox, 1923.

Jones, E. (1913). A simple phobia. In: *Papers on Psychoanalysis* (pp. 521–527). London: Balliere, Tindall & Cox, 1923.

Katan-Angel, A. (1937). Die Rolle der „Verschiebung" bei der Straßenangst. *Internationale Zeitschrift für Psychoanalyse*, 23: 376–392.

Kernberg, O. F. (1975). *Borderline Conditions and Pathological Narcissism*. New York: Jason Aronson.

Kernberg, O. F. (1976). *Object-Relations Theory and Clinical Psychoanalysis*. New York: Jason Aronson.

Khan, M. (1966). Role of phobic and counterphobic mechanism and separation anxiety in schizoid character formation. *International Journal of Psychoanalysis*, 47: 306–313.

Klemann, H., Kuda, M., & Massing, A. (1975). Phobie oder die Angst vor dem Dorf. *Zeitschrift für Psychosomatische Medizin und Psychoanalyse*, 21: 362–375.

Klüwer, K. (1974). Neurosentheorie und "Verwahrlosung". *Psyche, 28*: 285–309.

Kohut, H. (1971). *The Analysis of the Self: A Systematic Approach to the Psychoanalytic Treatment of Narcissistic Personality Disorders.* New York: International Universities Press.

Kohut, H. (1971). The analysis of the self. A systematic approach to the psychoanalytic treatment of narcissistic personality disorders. *Psychoanalytic Study of the Child*, Monograph No. 4. New York: International Universities Press.

Kohut, H. (1977). *The Restoration of the Self.* New York: International Universities Press.

König, K. (1976). Übertragungsauslöser—Übertragung—Regression in der analytischen Gruppe. *Gruppenpsychother. Gruppendyn, 10*: 220–232.

König, K. (1992). *Kleine psychoanalytische Charakterkunde.* Göttingen: Vandenhoeck & Ruprecht.

König, K. (1995a). *The Practice of Psychoanalytic Therapy.* Northvale, NJ: Jason Aronson.

König, K. (1995b). *Countertransference Analysis.* Northvale, NJ: Jason Aronson.

König, K. (2001). *Einführung in die psychoanalytische Interventionstechnik.* Stuttgart: Klett-Cotta.

König, K. (2004). *Charakter, Persönlichkeit und Persönlichkeitsstörung.* Stuttgart: Klett-Cotta.

König, K. (2007). *Transfer—Von der Psychotherapie in den Alltag.* Stuttgart: Klett-Cotta.

König, K. (2008). *Gruppenanalyse nach dem Göttinger Modell. Theoretische Grundlagen und praktische Hinweise.* Heidelberg: Mattes Verlag.

König, K. (2010). *Gegenübertragung und die Persönlichkeit des Psychotherapeuten.* Frankfurt/Main, Brandes und Apsel.

König, K. (2011). *Arbeit und Persönlichkeit.* Frankfurt/Main: Brandes und Apsel.

Kreische, R. (2004). Die phobische Kollusion. *Familiendynamik, 29*: 4–21.

Kuiper, P. C. (1973). *Die seelischen Krankheiten des Menschen.* Bern-Stuttgart: Huber und Klett.

Kulenkampff, C., & Bauer, A. (1960). Über das Syndrom der Herzphobie. *Der Nervenarzt, 31*: 443–454, 496–507.

Lewin, B. D. (1935). Claustrophobia. *Psychoanalytic Quarterly, 4*: 227–233.

Little, R. B. (1967). Spider phobias. *Psychoanalytic Quarterly, 36*: 51–60.

Little, R. B. (1968). The resolution of oral conflicts in a spider phobia. *International Journal of Psycho-Analysis, 49*: 492–494.

Lorenzer, A. (1970). *Sprachzerstörung und Rekonstruktion. Vorarbeiten zu einer Metatheorie der Psychoanalyse.* Frankfurt/Main: Suhrkamp.

Mahler, M. S. (1971). A study of the separation-individuation process and its possible application to borderline phenomena in the psychoanalytic situation. *Psychoanalytic Study of the Child, 26*: 403–424.

Mahler, M. S., Pine, F., & Bergman, A. (1975). *The Psychological Birth of the Human Infant. Symbiosis and Individuation*. New York: Basic Books.

Marks, I. M. (1970). Agoraphobic syndrome (phobic anxiety state). *JAMA Psychiatry (Archives of General Psychiatry), 23*: 538–553.

Marks, I. M., & Gelder, M. G. (1966). Different ages of onset in varieties of phobia. *American Journal of Psychiatry, 123*: 218–221.

Marks, I. M., & Herst, E. R. (1970). A survey of 1,200 agoraphobics in Britain. *Journal of Social Psychiatry, 5*: 16–24.

Meyer, J. -E. (1957). Studien zur Depersonalisation. II. Depersonalisation und Zwang als polare Störungen der Ich-Außenwelt-Beziehung. *Psychiatrische Neurologie, 133*: 63–79.

Meyer, J. -E. (1959). *Die Entfremdungserlebnisse. Über Herkunft und Entstehungsweisen der Depersonalisation*. Stuttgart: Thieme.

Miller, M. L. (1953). On street fear. *International Journal of Psycho-Analysis, 34*: 232–240.

Müller-Braunschweig, H. (1970). *Zur Genese der Ich-Störungen. Psyche, 24*: 657–677.

Nacht, S. (1966). The interrelationship of phobia and obsessional neurosis. *International Journal of Psycho-Analysis, 47*: 136–138.

Nagera, H. (1976). *Obsessional Neuroses. Developmental Psychopathology*. New York: Jason Aronson.

Nunberg, H. (1932). *Principles of Psychoanalysis: Their Application to the Neuroses*. New York: International Universities Press, 1955.

Oberndorf, C. P. (1950). The role of anxiety in depersonalization. *International Journal of Psycho-Analysis, 31*: 1–5.

Pittman, F. S., Langsley, D. G., & DeYoung, C. D. (1968). Work and school phobias: a family approach to treatment. *American Journal of Psychiatry, 124*: 1535–1541.

Post, S. C. (1964). The re-evocation of anxiety by its absence. *Psychoanalytic Quarterly, 33*: 526–535.

Quint, H. (1971). *Über die Zwangsneurose. Studie zur Psychodynamik des Charakters und der Symptomatik. Anmerkungen zur psychoanalytischen Behandlung*. Göttingen: Vandenhoeck & Ruprecht.

Renik, O. (1972). Cognitive ego function and the phobic symptom. *Psychoanalytic Quarterly, 41*: 537–555.

Renik, O. (1978). The role of attention in depersonalization. *Psychoanalytic Quarterly, 47*: 588–605.

Rhead, C. (1969). The role of pregenital fixations in agoraphobia. *Journal of the American Psychoanalytic Association, 17*: 848–861.

Richter, H. -E., & Beckmann, D. (1969). *Herzneurose*. Stuttgart: Thieme.

Riemann, F. (1961). *Grundformen der Angst*. München: Reinhardt.

Roth, M. (1959). The phobic anxiety-depersonalization syndrome. *Proceedings of the Royal Society of Medicine, 52*: 587–595.

Rubinfine, D. L. (1966). Comment on Mr. Khan's paper. *International Journal of Psycho-Analysis, 47*: 314–318.

Ruddick, B. (1961). Agoraphobia. *International Journal of Psycho-Analysis, 42*: 537–543.

Rudolf, G. (1977). *Krankheiten im Grenzbereich von Neurose und Psychose*. Göttingen: Vandenhoeck & Ruprecht.

Rycroft, C. (1968). *Anxiety and Neurosis*. London: Penguin.

Salzman, L. (1968). Obsessions and phobias. *International Journal of Psychiatry, 6*: 451–468.

Sandler, J., & Sandler, A. M. (1994). The past unconscious and the present unconscious; a contribution to a technical frame of reference. *Psychoanalytic Study of the Child, 49*: 276–292.

Sandler, J. & Sandler, A. -M. (1998). Internal Objects Revisited. London: Karnac.

Sarnoff, C. A. (1970). Symbols and symptoms. Phytophobia in a two-year-old girl. *Psychoanalytic Quarterly, 39*: 550–562.

Schafer, R. (1968). *Aspects of Internalization*. New York: International Universities Press.

Schultz-Hencke, H. (1951). *Lehrbuch der analytischen Psychotherapie*. Stuttgart: Thieme.

Segal, H. (1954). A note on schizoid mechanisms underlying phobia formation. *International Journal of Psycho-Analysis, 35*: 238–241.

Skynner, A. C. R. (1974). School phobia: a reappraisal. *British Journal of Medical Psychology, 47*: 1–16.

Snaith, R. P. (1968). A clinical investigation of phobias. *British Journal of Psychiatry, 114*: 673–697.

Sperling, M. (1971). Spider phobias and spider fantasies: a clinical contribution on the study of symbol and symptom choice. *Journal of the American Psychoanalytic Association, 19*: 472–498.

Steckel, W. (1924). *Störungen des Trieb—und Affekterlebens. 1. Nervöse Angstzustände und ihre Behandlung*. Berlin-Wien: Urban & Schwarzenberg.

Sterba, E. (1935). Excerpt from the analysis of a dog phobia. *Psychoanalytic Quarterly, 4*: 135–160.

Stiemerling, D. (1973). Analyse einer Spinnen—und Monsterphobie. *Zeitschrift für Psychosomatische Medizin und Psychoanalyse, 19*: 327–345.

Stierlin, H. (1971). Die Funktion innerer Objekte. *Psyche, 25*: 81–99.

Streeck, U. (1978). Bericht über die psychoanalytische Therapie eines Patienten mit narzißtisch-phobischer Charakterneurose. (unpublished).

Studt, H. H. (1974). Psycho—und Somatoneurosen im Vergleich: Angstneurose/Phobie—Asthma bronchiale. Eine psychosomatische Erkundungsstudie. University of Freiburg: Habilitation thesis.

Studt, H. H. (1984). Zur Ätiopathologie der Angstneurose und Phobie. In: U. Rüger (Ed.), *Neurotische und reale Angst*. Göttingen: Vandenhoeck & Ruprecht.

Terhune, W. (1949). The phobic syndrome: a study of 86 patients with phobic reactions. *Archives of Neurology and Psychiatry, 62*: 162–172.

Tucker, W. I. (1956). Diagnosis and treatment of the phobic reaction. *American Journal of Psychiatry, 112*: 825–830.

Wangh, M. (1959). Structural determinants of phobia: a clinical study. *Journal of the American Psychoanalytic Association, 7*: 675–695.

Weiss, E. (1935). Agoraphobia and its relation to hysterical attacks and to traumas. *International Journal of Psycho-Analysis, 16*: 59–83.

Weiss, E. (1953). Federn's ego psychology and its application to agoraphobia. *Journal of the American Psychoanalytic Association, 1*: 614–628.

Weiss, E. (1957). Ichstörungen bei der Agoraphobie und verwandten Erscheinungen im Lichte der Federnschen Ichpsychologie. *Psyche, 11*: 286–307.

Weiss, E. (1964). *Agoraphobia in the Light of Ego Psychology*. New York: Grune & Stratton.

Weiss, E. (1966). The psychodynamic formulation of agoraphobia. *Forum der Psychoanalyse, 1*: 378–386.

Weissman, P. (1966). The counterphobic state and its objects. *International Journal of Psycho-Analysis, 47*: 486–491.

Westphal, C. (1872). Die Agoraphobie; eine neuropathische Erscheinung. *Archiv fur Psychiatrie und Nervenkrankheiten, 3*: 138–161.

WHO (World Health Organisation), UNAIDS (1992). *The ICD-10 Classification of Mental and Behavioural Disorders: Clinical Descriptions and Therapeutic Guidelines*. Geneva: WHO.

Willi, J. (1972). Die angstneurotische Ehe. *Der Nervenarzt, 43*: 399–408.

Winnicott, D. W. (1953). Transitional objects and transitional phenomena. *International Journal of Psycho-Analysis, 34*: 89–97.

Winnicott, D. W. (1966). *The Maturational Processes and the Facilitating Environment: Studies in the Theory of Emotional Development*. New York: International Universities Press.

Zetzel, E. R. (1953). The traditional psychoanalytic technique and its variations. *Journal of the American Psychoanalytic Association, 1*: 526–537.

INDEX

64   INDEX